My Life of
Poems

Sean Michael McCarthy

authorHOUSE®

AuthorHouse™ UK
1663 Liberty Drive
Bloomington, IN 47403 USA
www.authorhouse.co.uk
Phone: 0800.197.4150

Published by AuthorHouse 04/21/2016

ISBN: 978-1-5246-3204-5 (sc)
ISBN: 978-1-5246-3205-2 (hc)
ISBN: 978-1-5246-3225-0 (e)

Print information available on the last page.

Contents

Happiness is like a fast moving train.

Rarely does it pull up at your station and invite you to climb aboard.

When it does, be sure that you jump on quickly and hold on tight.

That train will not stop for long and before you know it will speed off into your destiny.

Hold tight and hold fast as that train speeds around bends and clatters over bumps in an attempt to shake loose your grip and throw you from what could have been the ride of your life.

If this should be so then worry not.

Do not despair.

For I am along-side the track and I will always pick you up and dust you off.

I will attend to your bumps and scrapes of hurt and sorrow and soothe your remorse of failure.

I shall then offer you my hand to steady your stride and together we will walk the tracks until the train comes around again.

What follows are some poems written along my journey.

Some were written as I rode my destiny train, others as I fell from it and many as I walked along the track waiting for it to come around again.

Some are dark, some are deep and others loving. Some speak of loss and some are full of hurt. Some are full of joy and others are fun and slightly quirky.

They all offer hope, well; at least they did to me when I wrote them.

Enjoy.

[Just a small self-observation, I kind of think as I go along the poems get better. At the start they seem very raw compared to the ones at the end. I put this down to practise makes perfect progression].

Sean Michael McCarthy

1. Grass so green.

I saw you walk along the fence,
and watched you leave it made no sense.
You told me that you thought you'd seen,
some other grass that looked green.

You climber the fence then jumped on down,
said our grass faded brown.
But now that you've been gone a while,
you walk my fence in endless mile.

Looking back where once you'd been,
you see my grass that looks so green.
Without you here to tread it down,
the grass this side is no longer brown.

It's deep and lush so green and bright,
It makes you think your choice not right.
Many others that walk my fence,
agree your choice just made no sense.

You jumped to where you once had been,
just because that side played keen.
The trust you showed it got abused,
no longer wanted once played and used.

I walk my fields all by myself,
In grass that's green I have great wealth.
It's soft and deep so rich and lush,
to invite another there is no rush.

Another would my grass tread down,
and start it looking flat and brown.
For only one this grass I grow,
soul mate destiny these seeds I sow.

When my fields she has seen,
she will know for her my grass grows green.
Come climb my fence I'll help you down,
the fields we walk shall never brown.

2. Angels look down.

Angels look down on us from above,
early they choose the ones they will love.
Short is the time they leave us to see,
love given easy kindness for free.

Angels look down on us from above,
pure as the flight of white feathered dove.
Too soon they are taken up past the sun,
touched by the loss each everyone.

Angels look down on us from above,
holes in the heart where once sat the love.
Taken too early taken too soon,
up past the stars and over the moon.

High up in heaven and free from all strife,
world full of wonder from such a short life.
Left with the memories so full of love,
Angels look down on us from above.

3. The clock screams.

The clock screams tick to the echoed tock,
as I close the door and slide the lock.
My mind is racing with past wrong deeds,
guilt and sadness in a frenzy feeds.

Mirror so frosted by hot waters steam,
living the nightmare of a broken down dream.
Blurred sad reflection stares blankly back,
red Demon with horns clung tight to my back.

Eyes full of sadness no empathy,
soulless expression in mirror of me.
Heart so numbing, beating in pain,
moments turn calm as tensions drain.

Waters hotness soothes sets free,
sliding in under, shoulder then knee.
The clock screams tick to the echoed tock,
handle rattles on door found locked.

Mumbled questions on how long I take,
curt the retort of for goodness sake.
No peace and quiet, nor sanctuary,
always crowding and rushing me.

I long for quiet and restful sleep,
that silent dark of peaceful keep.
With one deep cut can come escape,
rescue soul from turmoil's rape.

Sean Michael McCarthy

Steaming waters turn crimson red,
as soothing bubbles submerge my head.
That echoed tock to the screamed out tick,
the door now knocking the urgent quick.

The moment passes by once more,
my dripping feet upon the floor.
Life continues its struggled race,
I open door to questioning face.

The room now vacant please feel free,
I step out from my sanctuary.
Leave behind that steamed up place,
whose mirror sees another face.

Steam fades away on passing breeze,
as back to living life I ease.
Such deep dark thoughts once more to hide,
horned red Demon is cast aside.

Back to living the new game plan,
make life as happy as I can.
I hear the ticking of the clock,
feel vibrations of echoed tock.

Reaper Grim he does withdraw,
top of list not me no more.
Perhaps intended, and happenstance,
or Guardian Angel with 2nd chance.

I lay in bed in my lonely room,
tick and tock the endless tune.
Tomorrow brings another day,
will good fortune come my way.

Depressions sadness came and past,
visits often but short time last.
Should you see my door on lock,
if you hear my echoed tock.

Please don't leave me by myself,
to stare at razor on the shelf.
Try the handle knock the door,
set my feet upon the floor.

Snap my mind from thoughts so deep,
interrupt Grim Reapers sweep.
Banish Demons with your knock,
clock screams tick to echoed tock.

4. Destiny's path.

Destiny calls us down winding lane,
leads us from pleasure takes us to pain.
So many choices but pick only one,
just take a step and decision is done.

Keep looking forward no glances back,
branches grow over to cover your track.
Burden of life is one heavy load,
carried down paths in search of the road.

A feeling of lost or choices made wrong,
go back to change with hindsight we long.
No return trip for that it's too late,
keep moving forward to close in on fate.

All paths all choices amount to the same,
whatever the route, path, road or lane.
Eventually merge at same end you see,
no matter the journey it's all destiny.

5. Does the world.

Does the world stop turning as I sit and stare,
with no thoughts of me, not even a care.
Mind lost in moments of past lives gone wrong,
pulled into memory by a yesterday song.

So easy to see all the bad choices made,
hindsight reveals all the clues that were laid.
Blind hearts of lovers once living the dream,
life full of perfect or so it did seem.

Does the world stop turning frozen still as a rock,
alone in my bedroom the handle on lock.
Times lost forever should better of spent,
pretend hopes and dreams you falsely me lent.

A fool and his money easily parted and used,
faith, love and trust betrayed and abused.
Does the world stop turning if eyes remain shut,
all those that cared from my life you have cut.

Some tried to warn where there's smoke follows fire,
with back turned in anger I judge them all liar.
Caught in your web with no struggle for free,
certain you couldn't serve cruel hurt to me.

Greatest of lovers, in that previous life,
stabbed in the back, by betrayals sharp knife.
Does the world even notice the beat of one heart,
will stars keep on shining as life falls apart.

Sean Michael McCarthy

Guardian Angels whisper warnings unheard,
friends pleas ignored I thought them absurd.
I felt it and knew it but chose to ignore,
broken heart drips pools puddle on floor.

My eyes are now fixed in distant dead stare,
a soul lost of dreaming with heart now laid bare.
Belief, faith and trust were once my strong shield,
stripped like the harvest on locust plagued field.

Does the world keep running now I'm out of the race,
is the sunshine like diamonds through tears on my face.
What why and if are the questions I reach,
is it Karma that delivers harsh lesson to teach.

If so then pray tell me of why I deserve,
to be thrown such a ball of painful hard curve.
Hurt before anger and then bitterness,
nobody deserves a life of such mess.

Does the world still exist if closed to my mind,
from depressions dark pit will escape I soon find.
I look to the heavens my heart heaves a sigh,
and ask the Lord questions of me again why.

Was I not loving, caring and good,
did I not always behave as I should.
The years now feel wasted back to square one,
alone with my hindsight of things should have done.

Does the world still want me what part can I play,
I need some direction and purpose to stay.
High are my walls my protection from pain,
afraid of the losing too scared of the game.

Nothing can heal me but the passing of time,
just keep on walking and all will be fine.
Eyes on horizon keep looking ahead,
once left this life then long the time dead.

One day will dawn in time all hurts heal,
escape all past nightmares live dream that is real.
Once more enjoy the laughter and play,
does the world keep on turning for my on this day.

6. How Angels earn their wings.

I stand atop my cliff and stare,
the pain will end if I just dare.
To take a step or maybe two,
the only thing I have to do.

Icy fingers of the breeze,
ruffles hair and scatters leaves.
Cool wet trails upon my cheek,
I dare not move I cannot speak.

Guardian Angel up above,
attention caught for pity's love.
I stand atop my cliff and see,
a world continued without me.

A final breath I draw in deep,
as I prepare my soul to leap.
Gulls shrill swirl above my head,
do it jump we want you dead.

I stand atop my cliff so high,
single star in clear cool sky.
The waves below hypnotic call,
rolling gently await my fall.

Just one step and woe will vanish,
torments end and turmoil's banish.
Life flashed by of lived in world,
time slows still from cliff top hurled.

The rocks below they rush up fast,
all moments froze to forever last.
Waves stand still like hills of glass,
heartbeats stop not one does pass.

I stand atop my cliff alone,
hard rocks are yet to smash up bone.
Did I jump why don't I fall,
what power silenced gulls harsh call.

I should have hit the rocks to smash,
cool waves greet to life's last dash.
I stand atop my cliff again,
wondering what, how and when.

Who's that stood right next to me,
are you an Angel can it be.
You take my hand and lead the way,
and show me where my body lay.

On cold hard rock with face all smashed,
this is how all hopes are dashed.
Spirit lost and all alone,
from bloodstained pocket rings my phone.

In that instant ring we go,
re-live life like fast slide show.
With all its wonder laughs and love,
as seen by Angels up above.

Good deeds done and difference made,
family friends and kids that played.
I stand atop my cliff and look,
through life of wonders favourite book.

No sadness seen no bad deed done,
just lots of love and times of fun.
You make me see with hindsight eyes,
so many that care to hear my cries.

My children dear so hurt and sad,
left to life without their dad.
Oh no dear God what did I do,
I see it now so clear and true.

The deed I done I wish had not,
too late to get back all I forgot.
I stand atop my cliff and stare,
rocks below but I'm not there.

Again I hear the seagulls cry,
what happened then in blink of eye.
Was it real or moments dream,
truly have I an Angel seen.

My step mid-air I now withdraw,
I feel your touch I glow in awe.
You came to me in moments need,
bid me follow your guiding lead.

My life redeemed another chance,
I turn and run with skip in dance.
Away from cliff and rocks that smash,
to world of living with gladly dash.

Back to life where I belong,
Angels showed the choice was wrong.
Decision made the best by far,
new eyes to see all that you are.

You showed me true achieved your goal,
sent from heaven to save my soul.
Moonlit sky and silver star,
nothing now my way shall bar.

A Guardian Angel just for me,
came to earth and set me free.
Free from worry and all the doubt,
made me see what life's about.

Job complete and passed the test,
returned to heaven for glory rest.
Heavens bell hear how it rings,
my Angel given brand new wings.

7. Nothing to say.

You've got nothing to say,
you just walk away.
The price that I pay,
for feeling this way.

My heart that you keep,
the tears that I weep.
With faith I did leap,
whilst falling so deep.

Love don't come cheap,
engaged tone phone beep.
As you I do seek,
for words just to speak.

Of knees gone all weak,
heart strings you tweak.
You've got nothing to say,
you just leave me this way.

All secrets soon leak,
like tears down my cheek.
Submissive and weak,
no longer unique.

My kisses run dry,
the harder I try.
No star in my sky,
the more you walk by.

You've got nothing to say,
my heart that you slay.
Forget not this day,
my love thrown away.

I text no reply,
keep asking you why.
Don't leave me alone,
just answer your phone.

My heart was no loan,
come back to our home.
Cupids arrow did fly,
our love mustn't die.

If only you'd try,
my hearts heavy sigh.
Can't make it alone,
no Queen to my throne.

Your true colours shown,
from nest you have flown.
You've got nothing to say,
don't end it this way.

The price big to pay,
why did you stray.
I miss how you moan,
in your ecstasy tone.

True feelings get shown,
whilst legs are wide thrown.
I stand watching you,
you fade from my view.

Know not what to do,
I just have no clue.
It looks like we're through,
is there somebody new.

I beg you please stay,
don't throw all away.
A year to the day,
that you walked away.

You text me to say,
hello there and hey.
Like to talk if you may,
can we meet up today.

A year of depression,
and Doctors couch session.
Of cleansing my soul,
and achieving that goal.

I made it you see,
of your spell I broke free.
So trump card I play,
this dog has his day.

For feelings I lack,
so I turn my back.
I've got nothing to say,
and I just walk away.

8. You said.

You said you love me would never leave,
you said forever made me believe.
You said my trust you'd never betray,
you said your eyes never would stray.

You said with me you'd found Mr Right,
you said all this as you held me tight.
You said that I was the best ever had,
you said my love made your heart feel glad.

You said I'm a knight in bright shining armour,
you said us meeting was destinies Karma.
You said I made you feel safe and secure,
you said your love was honest and pure.

You said commitment for the rest of your life,
you said you wanted a husband for wife.
You said I filled you with lust and desire,
you said all these words were you just a liar.

You said your love you would no longer hide,
you said you loved me on that cycle ride.
You said you'd fallen in love oh so deep,
you said your heart was mine to safe keep.

You said that I was your best ever friend,
you said your soul I did capture and mend.
You said so much that I believed true,
you said together we'd see all life through.

You said you were different not like the rest,
you said given time you'd prove yourself best.
You said that my mouth had the softest sweet lips,
you said all our kisses caused butterfly flips.

You said just my smile would fill you with lust,
you said please be yours and promise I must.
You said it all and gave my heart hope,
you said forever if certain I'd cope.

You said you promised so now tell me why,
you said you'd never in silence walk by.
You said we would always most certain be friends,
you said on your oath no matter what ends.

You said you can't handle a guy always nice,
you said I should try nasty just once or twice.
You said all your friends had finally been told,
you said no more hiding and nothing back hold.

You said love was wanted not no strings fun,
you said that I was the long searched for one.
You said you were tired of acting the clown,
you said it was time that you settled down.

You said that your love was a real true thing,
you said I should offer a gold diamond ring.
You said so much when stood face to face,
you said so many lies in our lovers embrace.

You said it in writing in letters read through,
you said that meant it and I should trust you.
You said that the world is full of players and cheat,
you said it, I know, you're the biggest to meet.

9. Every 2nd.

Every 2nd thought through my mind is your name,
each beat of my heart brings me pain.
Every 2nd face in the crowd I walk through,
each voice that I hear sounds like you.

Every 2nd breath that I take brings your scent,
each place that I go we once went.
Every 2nd dream that I have brings your smile,
each step that I take widens mile.

Every second past a moment lost without friend,
each turn that we took brought dead end.
Every 2nd best I became as you played me,
each thought I now have is to stay free.

Every 2nd cloud hung so grey silver lining,
each moment lived a heaven sent and divine thing.
Every 2nd dream that you dream you will find me,
each and every plan that you wouldn't let be.

Every 2nd tear that you cry slow drips blood red,
each every heart that you break and then leave dead.
Every 2nd thing that you say is cruel harsh word,
each step away from your grip is move forward.

Every 2nd day feelings fade the magic can't last,
each week turns to month then a year past.
Every 2nd face in the crowd shows me warm smile,
each look my way I now know liking my style.

Every 2nd choice I now make is the right one,
each every chance to fill my life with good fun.
Every second counts in the quest to quench a loves thirst,
each 2nd place Karma states deserves to come first.

Sean Michael McCarthy

10. 3rd time lucky.

I never thought I'd ever meet,
a girl to make my life complete.
I think of all I've done and seen,
like distant memory forgotten dream.

Sat alone and lost in space,
people watching for your face.
If I could have the time again,
do things different I would then.

I'd listen to the words you say,
and make things turn another way.
I'd take my time with fine romance,
out on dates with long slow dance.

I'd let you see me clear and true,
as your heart I'd try to woo.
Not just laughs or no strings fun,
long term lovers and the one.

I left it late for such words,
you fill my heart with humming birds.
They sing a tune so pure and clear,
how I long to hold you near.

Back once more and in my arms,
to have it so I'll try all charms.
I'll even wish upon a star,
you're just so perfect as you are.

And if my wishes do succeed,
I'll be the one and all you need.
Worth a go so let's be plucky,
give a chance for 3rd time lucky.

11. Small steps.

How quick we fall how fast we go,
from the highest high to the lowest low.
The smiles are gone replaced by frown,
head hung low with eyes kept down.

Small steps we take to who knows where,
where we arrive we just don't care.
In aimless trek with thoughts lost deep,
what reasons for the tears we weep.

Is the answer plain to see,
was it you or was it me.
Was timing wrong and all too good,
no chance was given to things that could.

There is no answer to questions asked,
the moment lost the chance has passed.
Small steps we take along the path,
forget the sad and false fake laugh.

The time was short and all too brief,
no chance discover the love beneath.
The sun shines down and then comes rain,
to warm the heart and wash the pain.

Is the answer plain to see,
was it you or was it me.
Was timing wrong and all too good,
no chance was given to things that could.

To all good things there comes an end,
when nothing remains, not even a friend.
All through life comes joy and pain,
with time again who'd choose the same.

Some mistakes triumphs and woe,
change nothing just leave it so.
Small steps we take yes this is true,
it's all that's left for us to do

12. How magic ends.

My eyes are open yet do not see,
I can't believe what's come to be.
A heart so empty how can it beat,
head hung low no eyes to meet.

Lonely footprints upon the sand,
nobody reaching to take my hand.
That moment special for which hearts pine,
when lovers fingers do inter-twine.

We did so much in short sweet space,
I miss the smile upon your face.
Once walked tall with head in cloud,
we're together the shout out loud.

To steal a kiss or maybe two,
Is what we both just longed to do.
You liked my laugh I loved your smile,
I thought you'd stay a longer while.

Came the moment all hearts dread,
I could not believe the words you said.
You sent a message to my phone,
it's over now you're on your own.

No face to face no reason why,
no parting hug or tear goodbye.
I stare at words that you have sent,
and wonder where the magic went.

Was it stolen or did it die,
look to heaven and ask God why.
All seemed great and all felt good,
romance was blooming as it should.

Out of blue you changed your mind,
sure feels cruel this being kind.
Did doubts creep in and feet get cold,
I treated you like dust of gold.

At very first seed of doubt,
you ran away and chickened out.
You now avoid all favoured place,
too scared that there you'll see my face.

I hear you think the reasons good,
no meet in person like you should.
All magic moments and wonders seen,
now forgot like faded dream.

No parting words or wished good luck,
just cast aside no give a fuck.
Damaged deep by once close friend,
shameful way for the magic end.

13. Lost dreams.

Mornings dawning stretching and yawning,
dreams of wonder whilst duvet under.
Sleepy eyes so tired and grainy,
check outside to see if rainy.

Bare feet pad across the floor,
down the stairs and through the door.
Shoulders slumped with tea pot steaming,
grasping shadows of what was dreaming.

Cold harsh world of shock awoken,
words of love that go unspoken.
Mornings dawning stretching and yawning,
steaming water into pots are pouring.

Lost the grasp of dreams that mattered,
fragment pieces on floor now shattered.
Stare across my empty table,
life once lived all turned to fable.

Thinking back when things were good,
when next to me you always stood.
Those hopes and dreams you tore to tatters,
a sense of loss of all that matters.

Life goes on and time will heal,
pinch myself to test if real.
Mornings dawning stretching yawning,
all ok the pretence we're fawning.

Sitting staring lost in ponder,
the wonder if the stars shine yonder.
Life continues with heavy trudge,
don't look back abandon grudge.

All things happen for a reason,
hearts turn cold like winter season.
Love turned off once more alone,
crawl back into safety zone.

Behind my walls no stress for me,
free of hurt when alone you be.
Sleeps escape stretching yawning,
soul at peace 'til mornings dawning.

14. I close my eyes.

I close my eyes and dare to dream,
and think of all I've done and seen.
I've been a lover and a friend,
had a start that found an end.

I've had a laugh been made to cry,
asked God when and pleaded why.
I'm sometime right but often wrong,
I try my best to get along.

Obey the law but break some rules,
suffer not the many fools.
I do not judge nor can complain,
enjoyed my pleasure felt the pain.

Exist in verse and dwell in song,
the things we do to get along.
I know some things but know not all,
I stand up strong yet sometimes fall.

My heart has loved and all was lost,
in life regrets I pay the cost.
I close my eyes and dare to dream,
and think of all I've done and seen.

Sean Michael McCarthy

15. If.

If I said sorry would you care,
if I cry will you be there.
If I stumble will you me catch,
if we nurture can love hatch.

If I give key to my hearts door,
if all then fails will you try once more.
If I forget will you remind,
if I get lost will you come find.

If I am honest will you then lie,
if I keep promise will you then try.
If I stay will you try to go,
if I say yes will you say no.

If I jump will you help me fly,
if I cry will you tears wipe dry.
If I give all will you take and take,
if I find fault will you admit mistake.

If I get stuck will you pull me through,
if I lose direction will you give a clue.
If I have no answer will you en-light,
if I offer arms will you hug me tight.

If I give my heart will you safe keep,
if I am tired will you guard my sleep.
If I am wrong will you prove right,
if I throw the towel will you then fight.

If I said sorry will you care,
if I get lonely will you be there.
If I commit will you say we're done,
if you then regret too late I've run.

16. Wasted mornings.

Roosters crow at daylights dawning,
sleepy children stretch whilst yawning.
Dragon breath mists on breeze dispersing,
milkman postman stood conversing.

Chink of sunlight breaks horizon,
out on lines the washing dries on.
Cows meander to meadows gate,
for early milking the patient wait.

Things that happen whist most asleep,
lost in dreams from counting sheep.
Early mornings land of wonder,
under duvets lost in slumber.

Bench in parks so quiet and empty,
golden leaves that float down gently.
By time you wake and start to yawning,
birds and bees are long past dawning.

Finally up and on your way,
farmer Giles through half his day.
Life passes by so very fast,
in blink of eye the season's past.

Wasted mornings in bed you lay,
sleeping half your life away.
Show the world that you are in it,
open eyes to every minute.

Sean Michael McCarthy

17. Single Sundays.

I am awake another day,
night time slumbers stretched away.
Dreams of wonder fading so,
body moving tired and slow.

Curtains drawn to sky so blue,
wondering what today to do.
List of things you must get done,
single Sunday's not much fun.

First a shower then cup of tea,
two bits of toast or sometimes three.
Eyes so grainy feeling sad,
wish last night's beer not had.

Sunday papers read the sport,
goalies beaten cricketers caught.
To the pub for pint or two,
usual rituals we all do.

Walk the dog along the beach,
lovers stroll with hands to reach.
Single Sundays aren't much fun,
if someone special you have none.

Children's laughter in the park,
dogs fetch sticks with happy bark.
Couples riding side by side,
on their Sunday cycle ride.

Back to home my footprints lead,
into bed to maybe read.
Shall I doze the day away,
no commitments for me this day.

As my eyes through pages sift,
closing slowly my mind's adrift.
Those dreams of wonder wanted back,
on single Sundays it's what I lack.

18. Parting.

I thought my heart would burst with pain,
you left me standing in the rain.
Our time was short and all too brief,
with endings comes the hurt and grief.

We had some laughs and lots of fun,
it came to end when just begun.
You need to know and have to see,
what it is you've done to me.

I may feel sad low and glum,
I won't regret the things we done.
You filled my days with laugh and smile,
memories that stay a long, long while.

Old friend of mine no longer near,
I'll think of you and shed a tear.
I'm standing here with no regret,
in the rain and getting wet.

19. Footprints past.

Life can be lonely,
when you walk on your own.
Nobody to text,
no calls to your phone.

A solitary trail,
of footprints in sand.
Lead to my feet,
as alone I do stand.

Waves roll in slowly,
upon gold sandy shores.
Erasing the trail,
that's single and yours.

The path we once walked,
washed away clean.
Smooth sands ahead,
the future unseen.

Standing and staring,
at distant horizon.
Knowing not what,
my destiny has eyes on.

Cool waves that soothe,
all hurts of the past.
Wiping from memory,
the pain at long last.

Waters retreat,
leave pristine clear beach.
The way is all clear,
new future to reach.

No looking back,
at trails left behind.
Keep moving forward,
with never the mind.

We all leave some shadow,
cast on the land.
Old trails of sorrow,
in yesterday's sand.

Many the reasons,
to tempt your glance back.
Keep moving forward,
along destiny track.

The past is all over,
it's been and long gone.
Leave buried in dust,
the broken and wrong.

The living is now,
this moment we speak.
Today and tomorrow,
not lost in last week.

The future uncertain,
of this there's no doubt.
Live life for the moment,
is what it's about.

Stride forward with purpose,
brave heart in hand.
As Guardian Angels,
beside you will stand.

Take all good moments,
forget all the bad.
Carry the laughter,
drop all the sad.

Like footprints in sand,
come end of day.
Waves of contentment,
wash sadness away.

Walk tall and determined,
along chosen beach.
With confident strides,
to destiny reach.

If life has a lesson,
for many unknown.
Live every day,
like King on your throne.

Sean Michael McCarthy

Fill days with laughter,
love and some fun.
Smile at the weather,
wind rain or sun.

If you should see me,
as I walk a beach.
Come walk beside me,
learn what I teach.

I'll show you some splendour,
not witnessed before.
Two trails of footprints,
we'll leave on the shore.

Into the sunset,
they meander and weave.
Searching out futures,
the past they both leave.

20. Midnight lovers.

My eyes wide open I am awake,
it takes a moment to bearings take.
In darkness shines the moonlit sky,
soft rhythm breaths and sleepy sigh.

With gentle caution I take a peek,
to check for access on what I seek.
You lay there naked deep in dream,
starlit twinkle of my eyes so keen.

Soft and naked so deep in sleep,
no clothe to hide your treasure keep.
With gentle hands I part your thighs,
heart beats eager for within what lies.

The only sound said beating heart,
eager trembles the keen to start.
I kiss and lick with tongue explore,
whilst in your dreams you yearn for more.

Your hips move slow in gentle grind,
who knows what dreams now flood your mind.
Lost in fantasy of passions lust,
body quivers to tongues quick thrust.

I do all gently so as not to wake,
in your sleep breaths sharp intake.
Gasping now but not there yet,
treasured keep so warm and wet.

I ease back up and lay beside,
moments scant before eyes are wide.
Oh my God are you awake,
such dreams of lust did I just take.

You lean in close and grab me tight,
find the thing you crave this night.
Midnight plan worked perfectly,
as you slide on top of me.

Gentle moans slow rocking sway,
you let your magic out to play.
Bodies hot kissing smothers,
timed perfection of midnight lovers.

21. Morning urge.

I lay awake and stare a while,
to watch you sleep it makes me smile.
It takes a minute maybe two,
before my watching wakens you.

I lean on down and gently kiss,
morning whispers pretty Miss.
You see the smile in eyes shine through,
and know in instant that I want you.

I feel the softness of your skin,
both minds desire the games begin.
Slow light kisses lips brush hip,
hands touch lightly curve of hip.

Mouth slides down so teasing slow,
excitement builds where will I go.
You lay back down upon the bed,
want you now the words unsaid.

I find your secret magic place,
gentle circles with tongue I trace.
You arch your back to draw me in,
release the magic let go begin.

In heartbeat moment you reach your peak,
body spasms you cannot speak.
You pull me up to lips find mine,
take me quick right now's the time.

Passion burning bright in eyes,
slide in gentle moans and sighs.
It isn't long before we find,
matching rhythm hypnotic grind.

Bodies merge to shudder shake,
as together we climax take.
Limbs entwined as souls they merge,
heavens bliss of mornings urge.

22. Hay fever.

Wake up sneezing with itchy eyes,
dreading days of clear blue skies.
Thumping head and tingling nose,
this is how hay fever goes.

Body aches with joints all stiff,
sneeze and cough with constant sniff.
Tablets taken nose spray as well,
must get through this living hell.

We love the summers adore the sun,
but hate the fever that spoils the fun.
Stuck indoors can't venture out,
I hate hay fever the common shout.

Those that mock and suffer not,
no understanding of what we've got.
It leaves you drained and feeling bad,
in a world that thinks us mad.

Wake up sneezing with itchy eyes,
each summer hears our anguished cries.
It's a curse if suffer you do,
dread the days of skies clear blue.

23. White winged butterfly.

Searching soul for guiding voice,
stuck decision confusing choice.
Inspiration flutters by,
guiding white winged butterfly.

Words of promise that you spoke,
taken back to leave heart broke.
Remembered like it was today,
that you turned and walked away.

All false dreams of which you spoke,
was it game or just cruel joke.
Did your words show true remorse,
or were they lies to smooth the course.

I sit alone and ask God why,
soft white wings go flutter by.
My words are lost I cannot speak,
salt the trails that stain my cheek.

Knees to chest I hug so tight,
what you've done just isn't right.
To the world once shouted loud,
next to me stood tall and proud.

How great you said it was to be,
in the arms of destiny.
You walked away with practised ease,
soft white wings on summer's breeze.

Not one glance back or tear in eye,
fluttered off with no goodbye.
I walk alone this summer's day,
lost in thoughts that guide my way.

Through flower meadow high on moor,
of life direction no longer sure.
Erratic dancers catch my eye,
guiding white winged butterfly.

It seems when sad or feeling down,
your wings appear to smooth my frown.
You dance and float on summer's breeze,
as if my soul you aim to please.

Spirit of hearts of loves passed by,
return to guide as butterfly.
For every choice so hard to do,
seems chose right when I see you.

Sometimes when lost and all alone,
soft white wings will guide me home.
In my thoughts with hearts deep sigh,
I fail to grasp all reasons why.

You filled my soul with lust desire,
words not true just played by liar.
Our time was full of words not meant,
the dream in ruin the magic spent.

Shining knight as once was seen,
rescue done soon fades the gleam.
I held you gently did I not,
how all you promised so soon forgot.

On hill up high I sit alone,
bees around buzz soothing drone.
Hover circles in endless search,
to hunt lost souls upon to perch.

Such complex lives of failed tries,
explain to me the ifs and whys.
As if by magic my thoughts you hear,
on gentle breeze you flutter near.

You know in me there is no harm,
alight your wings upon my palm.
Soft wings so white with tremor rest,
the path of flight your only test.

Lived in dance through good or bad,
a life too short for feeling sad.
No need to dwell on reasons why,
just float like white winged butterfly.

Sweet the taste of nectars power,
absorb the soul from every flower.
Erratic dance from tree to plant,
no knowledge of the why you can't.

Through wind and rain with morning chill,
brave the world and live life still.
Not glum or scared no woe is me,
wings catch breeze to float you free.

Sole purpose given to search out flower,
enjoy the taste from each soul's power.
Without a worry, just take the chance,
believe your faith in butterfly dance.

Wings from heaven what are your goals,
sent down to earth to find lost souls.
No longer sad no tears to cry,
saved by Angels white butterfly.

You lift my eyes the world to see,
rescued heart and set me free.
My stuck decision confusing choice,
whispered cure from Angel's voice.

You came to me to share Gods power,
the flutter down to save each flower.
The gentle breeze lifts wings to sky,
back to heaven white butterfly.

24. Life reflections

I stand before a mirror looking back at all to see,
I wonder if life inside is better there for me.
The patterns on the ceiling all merge and form a face,
am I such a pattern on some others ceiling place.

Are we specks throughout the cosmos floating random in the air,
do we cease in our existence if the Gods no longer care.
Does a heart give up it's beating when lost the will to live,
will an eye continue crying when dry of tears to give.

Have I made a difference on this side of the glass,
do I stir up your emotions when through your thoughts I pass.
How would it affect things had I never been,
would it make a difference had me the world not seen.

I stand before a mirror and stare into my eyes,
you stand silent looking back with no answer to my cries.
Trapped behind the glass always silent watching me,
aghast at all you witness through eyes of green envy.

You stand inside your mirror eternal statue looking out,
never to berate me, complain or moan and shout.
Just trapped forever longing for all that you can see,
froze inside the mirror no hopes of breaking free.

My life of woe and wonder the good as well as bad,
the freedom I've to live it the thing you've never had.
As I look into my mirror the one above the sink,
I catch your look of envy that makes me stop to think.

Splash my face with water feels refreshing and so cool,
no more wasting time in ponder like a bloody fool.
I'll turn and face this challenge of life of being me,
with knowledge that you watch me through eyes of jealousy.

Life this side is real, not reflection in a glass,
enjoy each every moment for quickly will it pass.
Fill it full of laughter, love and fun with glee,
so all Angels trapped in mirrors find it good to see.

25. Like a summers day.

Like a summer's day cooling breeze,
is how you make my worries ease.
Like a summer's day warming sun,
filled my world with love and fun.

Like a summer's day of clear blue sky,
you gave my life a reason why.
Like a summer's day long and bright,
we felt so good we felt so right.

Like a summer's day on golden sand,
perfect moments of holding hand.
Like a summer's day upon the beach,
to smile again you did me teach.

Like a summer's day of heavens bliss,
lips that touched in sweet first kiss.
Like a summer's day of bright warm shine,
I really thought that all was fine.

Like a summer's day so chilled and lazy,
feeling joys of smitten crazy.
Like a summer's day fine and dry,
a smile from you made all doubts die.

Like a summer's day we all enjoy,
magic moments of girl meets boy.
Like a summer's day with sunset glow,
if given chance such love could grow.

Like a summer's day that brings warm night,
if left to be then things just might.
Like a summer's day of which there's many,
no reason not to no not any.

Like a summer's day so few we had,
sweet memories of forever glad.
Like a summer's day of pure perfection,
spent with you and your affection.

Like a summer's day of sky so blue,
such pride and faith I put in you.
Like a summer's day to warm the heart,
I never dreamed that we would part.

Like a summer's day it had to end,
who will now, my broke heart tend.
Like a summer's day red sunset glow,
it saddens me to let you go.

Like a summer's day that fades from view,
I stand alone what now to do.
Like a summer's day that will never last,
our moment over the magic past.

26. Empty pillows.

I lay on my bed alone and I stare,
one empty pillow I see you're not there.
Single frame picture looks down upon me,
a moment so happy caught perfectly.

At breakfast table I now eat alone,
no morning love message to read on my phone.
I eat and I drink but no longer taste,
the chances we've lost to destiny waste.

Lock the front door and climb into car,
morning sun fades nights wished upon star.
Start up the engine with shudder and shake,
feeling so sad with heart full of ache.

Change my route taken to drive past your house,
nothing is stirring not even a mouse.
Work the day through to my well known routine,
not once am I noticed by no one get seen.

My head I keep low in quiet lost thought,
I remember the moment when my heart you caught.
The hours keep passing but minutes drag slow,
pain of this heartbreak I wish it would go.

Working day done it's time to head back,
appetite low so grab drive through snack.
I breathe I'm alive but barely exist,
I fade from all view like weak morning mist.

I park up the car once more I am home,
dread the inside with all the alone.
Up garden path slowly I walk,
neighbours hello lost desire no talk.

Into the lock I slide the brass key,
the very same one that you returned me.
Off come my shoes clothes to the floor,
how long will it hurt can't take any more.

Into the shower with water set cool,
hindsight berates me I cry like a fool.
Alone in my room all thoughts to myself,
frozen are moments in pictures on shelf.

The darkness draws out the night sky and star,
I can't help but wonder if happy you are.
Staring at ceiling in big empty bed,
lost in confusion from thoughts in my head.

Faint distant odours of forgotten perfume,
linger like ghosts in corners of room.
Drift off to sleep whilst asking God why,
softly the pillows catch tears that I cry.

Sleep finally claims my soul all alone,
slips from my hand your picture on phone.
In dreams I am happy with you by my side,
but magic is lost when eyes open wide.

Morning already a new day to start,
once more routine with hurt heavy heart.
I lay on my bed alone and I stare,
one empty pillow I see you're not there.

27. Free.

Free at last I am free at last,
what's gone before is lost and past.
Yesterday snow and dreams of last year,
melted away and no longer here.

Erased from my mind and faded from dream,
ousted from soul like never had been.
No longer your shadow will darken my path,
heart finally free and able to laugh.

Living life to the full moving free and so fast,
all feels so good when again free at last.

28. Free to fly.

Free to fly and free to soar,
you can't hold me down no more.
Free to laugh and have some fun,
no more worry if wrong I've done.

Free to skip and free to dance,
no more beggars for 2nd chance.
Free to walk and free to fly,
no lonely nights into pillow cry.

Free of worry and free of stress,
let it go and don't care less.
Free of orders and controlling laws,
free to make the whole world yours.

29. Someone.

I want someone to look at me,
love me unconditionally.
I want someone to just be mine,
not open to offers all of the time.

I want someone to take my hand,
spur of moment not tactic planned.
I want someone to say that word,
so all the world is sure they heard.

I want someone to hold at night,
pleased to finally get love right.
I want someone that's proud of me,
not to hide with secrecy.

I want someone stood by my side,
the fact we're lovers not to hide.
I want someone that tells no lies,
no deceit from fake false wolf cries.

I want someone to give a chance,
not to lead a merry dance.
I want someone who just wants me,
not string along two or three.

I want someone who likes my kiss,
when apart the soul to miss.
I want some to love me whole,
with dreams to match my life goal.

I want someone that's happy to be,
spotted together out publicly.
I want someone that speeds hearts beat,
doesn't lie and would never cheat.

I want someone with strength to stay,
not to run or trust betray.
I want someone that likes to laugh,
with wish to share the future path.

I want someone who's not afraid,
admit my arms at night she's laid.
I want someone that could eventual,
offer long term with true potential.

I want someone to stick and stay,
like a shadow on sunshine day.
I want someone to text reply,
not leave me hanging out to dry.

I want someone to I love you,
know it feel it mean it true.
I want someone keeps safe my heart,
not break or smash nor tear apart.

I want someone to share my world,
whilst watching films on sofa curled.
I want someone to in morning wake,
breakfast in bed with me to take.

I want someone just one will do,
wishing star oh please come true.
I want someone to look at me,
to give me love with all strings free.

30. Summer rains.

Summer came and then it went,
we long for days on beach we spent.
Clear blue skies without a cloud,
girls go topless where allowed.

Sun-cream hats and ice cream cones,
whole days spent outside of homes.
Freckles sprinkled upon your nose,
deep tanned skin with healthy glows.

Such was weather throughout June,
over quick and gone too soon.
July and August cloudy wet,
with wind thrown in as well I bet.

September may bring Indian summer,
if not unlucky what a bummer.
Every year we hope and dream,
for long hot summers as childhood seen.

We crave to hear that weather man,
utter words like hosepipe ban.
Every day we all ask why,
raindrops fall from summer sky.

No excuse and no good reason,
why August is the new wet season.
Give us sunshine no more rain,
one brings pleasure the other pain.

It matters not what's up above,
should we find a summer love.
Be it hot or wet and cold,
matters not when hearts behold.

Arms wrapped around in lovers reach,
stealing kisses on moonlit beach.
If raindrops fall upon your head,
not one is felt when love is said.

Dodging raindrops is great fun,
when moment shared with special one.
How we crave wet summer days,
so we can with lovers laze.

The weather matters not one bit,
when there's someone special to share it.
Days that end with sunset glows,
tomorrow nice the forecast shows.

A sunset deep red orange sky,
reflects perfection of lovers eye.
Tomorrow's sunny maybe might,
a sunshine day puts all wrongs right.

Wake up hearing raindrops patter,
onto windows splash 'n splatter.
Yet another summer day,
washed out with a rain stops play.

When you're loved up not alone,
you don't mind to stay at home.
If unlucky and you're just one,
staying in is just no fun.

Oh how it brings all folks together,
polite small talk of English weather.
Summer came and then it went,
we long for days on beach we spent.

31. Cheek pressed into grass.

With my cheek pressed into grass,
life's last breath in final gasp.
Upon sweet green the meadow field,
someone me I think just killed.

My eyes are wide and facing sky,
slow salty tears begin to cry.
Clouds float framed by rich deep blue,
what reasons for these things we do.

The hurts they fade and cease to ache,
my soul laid bare now Gods to take.
Birds in circles spiral high,
are they Angels in the sky.

The distant battle rages on,
my moment past my time has come.
Flashing by goes short lived life,
loving children doting wife.

My bloods slow soak into the land,
can't quite grasp or understand.
Only precious moments since,
running zigzags short fast sprints.

A single lonely loud sharp crack,
stabbing pain into my back.
Drilled in role position aim,
fingers tingle numb with pain.

With my cheek pressed into grass,
all my comrades running past.
Every soldier but me runs on,
has no one noticed I am gone.

The only sound I seem to hear,
heartbeat pumping pulses fear.
Speeding fast begins to slow,
my grip on life it starts to go.

Smell the earth the tree and flower,
senses boost of dying power.
Distant battle rages on,
man down comes the medics' song.

At last I see a friendly face,
quick check for my pulses race.
Please my wife and children tell,
my love and thoughts for them as fell.

Promise me right now you better,
pass to them this blood stained letter.
It's full of love and last goodbyes,
of how I'll watch from Angel's skies.

Fingers probing for my hurt,
cut away my crimson shirt.
For me by now there's no more pain,
no fight to lose or ground to gain.

With my cheek pressed into grass,
needled morphine from tube of glass.
At long last my wound is seen,
frantic effort with haste to clean.

Try to stop the steady flow,
as into earth my blood does go.
No longer feel I can hardly hear,
a shadow cast by Angels near.

All too often this is seen,
far too many there has been.
Heavens halls are full to brim,
every war will squash more in.

Angels stand and wait in queue,
sent to earth to guide souls through.
Through pearly gates to heavens hall,
before the Lord must pass us all.

Another soldier killed in battle,
in fields once full of grazing cattle.
In that distant now fading land,
medics comfort squeeze of hand.

Hang in there buddy his silent cry,
as tears of truth show clear the lie.
Can tell by shadow across his face,
he knows in heart he's lost this race.

With my cheek pressed into grass,
an Angel stops her slow walk past.
Despite the medics' efforts best,
my soul floats free from hole in chest.

Floats into my Angels hand,
time to guide me from this land.
From life of living the silent slip,
family photos' from pockets tip.

Please now don't you all be sad,
for efforts given I am glad.
If not for me here this day,
many innocents here could lay.

If I could ask for just one thing,
to make my soul in heaven sing.
On summer days yet to pass,
lay down your cheek against the grass.

Look up to heaven and clear blue sky,
remember all the reasons why.
Brave soldiers fight and many fall,
now stand as Angels in heavens hall.

32. Hearts to tend.

Life goes by so very fast,
hardly see our shadow cast.
Take for granted our every day,
shrug off memories that forever stay.

Magic moments lived and past,
did not know they were the last.
Ignore all words that lovers say,
dreaming in their arms you lay.

Road once straight meets sudden bend,
left alone in life to fend.
Comes a moment in blink of eye,
all contentment passes by.

Feel so broke no chance to mend,
as Angels gather hearts to tend.
Shattered world like storm blown sky,
eyes they see too late now cry.

Soul mate lover friend with pride,
cruelly taken from your side.
What we had was heavens bliss,
not 'til gone do truly miss.

Tears too frequent now to hide,
never has a heart so sighed.
Remember fondly last lingered kiss,
who'd of thought it could come to this.

What once was great fast turned bad,
happy heart left burst and sad.
Feels like dream was never real,
heart now gripped by talon steel.

Re-live the days of fun we had,
memory moments forever glad.
Cruel cards of fate so fast the deal,
time alone will soothe and heal.

A moral to all stories end,
lost you lover or best friend.
Sat alone under dark night sky,
hands together to pray ask why.

Don't leave your love too late to send,
no surrender hearts to Angels tend.
No answer for your questioned sigh,
feel no shame for tears you cry.

Memories stay the pain will end,
if you stumble lean on friend.
I'll hold you up and stand you tall,
always close for you to call.

Don't stagger blind in endless roam,
don't hide in darkness all alone.
No need to bare the weight of world,
shadow hide in corners curled.

If your Angel's too far to hear,
come to me and share your fear.
I'll loan an ear for you to bend,
pass to me your hearts to tend.

Sean Michael McCarthy

33. Rumbo.

Every time we see a bike it brings to mind your name,
every year this day arrives it gives to heart some pain.
Taken up from us so quick no chances for goodbye,
lifted up above the clouds by Angels in the sky.

Your smiling laugh we hear it still each time you come to mind,
it makes us pause lost in thought for reasons we can't find.
As the years fast drift by we're left with memory,
not lost or gone and not forgot your soul that God set free.

You're on a cloud without a care never growing old,
never said or feeling low no tiredness or cold.
When Rumbo drifts into your thoughts as often does with me,
fill your heart and your soul with happy memory.

34. When I close my eyes.

When I close my eyes in darkness deep,
I close my eyes and cannot weep.
When I close my eyes the things I dream,
I close my eyes to the world I've seen.

When I close my eyes my racing mind,
I close my eyes the peace I find.
When I close my eyes the darkness shroud,
I close my eyes to dreams allowed.

When I close my eyes it hurts the most,
I close my eyes to memories ghost.
When I close my eyes and fade to sleep,
I close my eyes all hearts will weep.

When I close my eyes the dreams I take,
I close my eyes I fear to wake.
When I close my eyes you still stand near,
I close my eyes not gone still here.

When I close my eyes and ask God why,
I close my eyes no last goodbye.
When I close my eyes it can't be true,
I close my eyes your time not through.

When I close my eyes I see last meet,
I close my eyes your hand shake greet.
When I close my eyes there's nothing wrong,
I close my eyes you haven't gone.

When I close my eyes in dream look back,
I close my eyes our long shared track.
When I close my eyes remember mate,
I close my eyes to heaven's gate.

When I close my eyes you're up above,
I close my eyes your life of love.
When I close my eyes I shall awake,
when you closed yours the Lord did take.

35. Kind heart slayer.

Some words of hurt they cut so deep,
for endless time the pain will weep.
Heart so broke the sad never end,
no horizon hope of sunshine send.

Weeks to month then years pass by,
memory fades the wrongs and why.
Miss the good the laughs and fun,
ignore the wounds from bad things done.

To love and lose they say is better,
hearts when dark write vengeful letter.
The void stands wide from good to bad,
cause all thoughts to linger sad.

To be betrayed by lovers end,
installs deep hurt to never mend.
Those walks on beach in summer sun,
and cycle rides so full of fun.

Picnics eaten on trips we took,
flick through mind like picture book.
Lazy Sunday our favourite day,
words we had no need to say.

We had it all with grass so green,
how happy life back then did seem.
Hindsight knowledge is now my gift,
through magic moments my mind does sift.

Signs are plenty and plain to see,
known by all but not by me.
Gut instinct screamed and got ignored,
senses lost in you adored.

Sean Michael McCarthy

All words spoken as truth I'd take,
made up lies and forgery fake.
Finally caught when mask did slip,
condemned by words leaked past your lip.

Soul destroyer and kind heart slayer,
the truth did oust the liar player.
You took my love my gifts and money,
whilst with another you thought it funny.

All around my world did crash,
thrown away like rotten trash.
My head held high in righteous stance,
ignore your please for second chance.

I gave you two then three and four,
enough is enough that's it no more.
You made your bed now in it lay,
shattered heart threw bits away.

In this life there's one thing certain,
karma notes who does the hurting.
It waits in shadows for chance to pounce,
pays back all to every ounce.

Watch on as I ignore your pleas,
when Karma fells you to your knees.
I'll praise the Lord for justice done,
turn my back and just walk on.

36. Winter fun.

Silent flakes float gently down,
make children smile like circus clown.
Crisp pure whiteness all around,
covers trees and blankets ground.

Hands pulled up inside of sleeves,
footprints that the robin leaves.
Like engines steaming through the snow,
our plumes of breath in billow show.

There's mistletoe for quick kiss stealing,
good will to all the common feeling.
Christmas comes just once a year,
chance to have all loved ones near.

A time once more for feeling young,
can't resist that snowball bung.
Winter nights with snow laid deep,
open fires to all warm keep.

Born again and feel alive,
build the biggest snowman strive.
A day off work and there's no school,
the whole world out as sledging fool.

We curse the winter for feeling cold,
as extra layers on we fold.
The search for bin lids old tea tray,
these things that we can use for sleigh.

We climb the hills to highest peak,
so out of breath we cannot speak.
When reaching top we wait our turn,
to be the fastest our secret yearn.

Tuck in feet and hold on tight,
some close eyes too scared for sight.
Whizzing down and facing fear,
blurring faces laugh and cheer.

In that moment there and then,
the whole world over aged just ten.
At end of day so tired and done,
remember days of winter fun.

37. Tired.

I'm tired of being lonely like a sparrow in the rain,
I'm tired of my heartbeats slow and full of pain.
I'm tired of always giving getting nothing in return,
I'm tired of life's harsh lessons from which I never learn.

I'm tired of lonely beach walks with no one by my side,
I'm tired of all the quitters who never really tried.
I'm tired of being lied to, cheated on, betrayed,
I'm tired of the waiting for the hurt to finally fade.

I'm tired of investing all faith and trust in you,
I'm tired of discovering all your words untrue.
I'm tired of building dreams to have you smash them down,
I'm tired of acting happy like a sad old circus clown.

I'm tired of always waiting for tomorrow's another day,
I'm tired of thinking true love has finally come my way.
I'm tired of always catching each and every fall,
I'm tired of your silence and your promises to call.

I'm tired of the radio that always plays our song,
I'm tired of that feeling that something will go wrong.
I'm tired of being needed but of never getting kept,
I'm tired of all the tears that you crocodile wept.

I'm tired of all the dreams that pass by in a haze,
I'm tired of having nothing to my soul amaze.
I'm tired of excuses not you it's down to me,
I'm tired of being told I treat you too kindly.

I'm tired of all the players you permit to part your thighs,
I'm tired of realization you're a snake the true disguise.
I'm tired of wasting time these months that eat up years,
I'm tired of all the paranoid all the stress and all the fears.

I'm tired of being abandoned left alone to fend,
I'm tired of the promise to always be a friend.
I'm tired of the journey keeps turning out the same,
I'm tired of being lonely like a sparrow in the rain.

38. Choices.

To walk around in lost despair,
to wonder if there's someone there.
With dreams that took another path,
tears can turn to happy laugh.

Some cruel hurt twist of destiny,
is this what fate had planned for me.
Why pick me and not some other,
insignificant for Karma's bother.

Life seems one big up-hill struggle,
confusion clouds my mind to muggle.
Lost in thoughts so deep and dreamy,
do the Angels even see me.

Paths lead left and to the right,
moving forward or back I might.
Stuck decision of confusing choice,
waiting for that guiding voice.

Head hung low my slow lost plod,
lost belief there is a God.
The future said already written,
twice as shy for once been bitten.

Good stands silent as evil goads,
tries to sway our chosen roads.
Crossroad confusion no signpost clear,
indecision that prompt the fear.

Sean Michael McCarthy

Quick glance back shows no trail travelled,
all life's threads at feet unravelled.
What to do what choice to make,
at passing faces my smile I fake.

Eyes wide open in dreamy stare,
loved ones see but do they care.
What's the point to all of life,
mother Father Husband Wife.

To walk around in lost despair,
life once great has lost its flare.
Does it matter what we choose,
heaven hell win or lose.

Will history know in a thousand years,
who stopped to carefully catch your tears.
All that matters is that you try,
to smile content as life slips by.

To do your best for you and others,
love fellow man like long lost brothers.
We walk a path lost deep in thought,
remembering smiles our eyes once caught.

Too many crossroads confusing choice,
devils whisper or Angel's voice.
This life we live is one big test,
heaven rewards those deemed the best.

When lost in dark the light is sought,
to righteous choice our soul is brought.
Be kind to friend or foe,
spread good deed the seed you sow.

Make the choice of right not wrong,
life world spirit in gracious song.
No secret formula for success,
some get it right most make a mess.

So when alone and lost in thought,
avoid the drag towards distraught.
Don't feel alone do not despair,
be assured that Angels care.

We walk through life on golden thread,
God weaves us born and cuts us dead.
Once our tapestry of life complete,
all Angels will at gates us meet.

39. Under covers.

Today is the day that's meant for all lovers,
to cuddle and kiss and spoon under covers.
For flowers and cards and breakfast in bed,
I love you words with meaning now said.

A sky full of arrows from cupids own bow,
deep seeds of love his good aim shall sow.
Cards are arriving hand writing disguised,
the sender the secret a question mark hides.

Flowers get given mostly roses of red,
words we all long for are finally said.
Meals out together remember to book,
across lighted candles the dreamy eyes look.

Soft music playing a beat for slow dance,
hug tight together this special romance.
Wearing best outfits best suit and new dress,
fingers stroke faces with gentle caress.

Comes once a year this day meant for lovers,
to spoon kiss and cuddle under the covers.
We sit on the doorstep awaiting the mail,
red hearted envelopes containing loves tale.

A story of lovers all soon to be,
hearts full of longing and dreams of happy.
Postman approaches sends spine a small shiver,
such eager excitement come on deliver.

The feeling inside is one of a kind,
loves perfect moments go racing through mind.
Insides all flutter with butterfly dance,
the sharing of magic Valentine of romance.

Everything's perfect all is just right,
never before has the sun shone so bright.
Life is all roses when shared with a lover,
to kiss spoon and cuddle under the cover.

40. Uncensored thoughts.

The world so full of hurt and greed,
starving children that cannot feed.
Mankind he is drowning in hurt and hate,
come to sense before chance is too late.

Evil acts under guise of good,
mans' compassion adrift like wood.
Conspiracy scandal murder mayhem,
standing alone will fail to stop them.

Like sheep in a field head hung low,
pretend not to see it just might go.
Pass on by not my concern,
too busy with money to spend and earn.

Picture box talking from corner it lies,
blocks out your mind like clouds do the skies.
Keeps you thinking a threat is near,
controls the world through false flag fear.

Governments acting like fairy tale knights,
claims of protection from wars and fights.
What lurks behind curtains in corners so dark,
pricks at the conscience we fail to hark.

Not my concern I don't want to know,
if I ignore it maybe might go.
This day and age it just isn't done,
to offer a hand of good Samaritan.

You think you are free to do all that you can,
fell for the ruse and trusted the spam.
The world is divided the choice between two,
what side you stand is all up to you.

Take closer look it's God or the Devil,
one side stands pure the other lays evil.
Long ancient battles fought many times,
forgotten as myths or lost nursery rhymes.

End game approached not if but when,
where will you run and get there what then.
Society stands like brain washed lost sheep,
no words of complaint awareness asleep.

The true words of God in stories once told,
no longer get written in the Bibles we hold.
Those greedy in power so worried of loss,
destroyed man-kinds saviour via nail and cross.

For too long all people have abandoned free choice,
surrendered their minds to the media's voice.
If it's not on the telly it's surely not true,
I've knowledge of Jesus what about you.

The world going crazy with greed on its lips,
four horsemen come riding apocalypse.
No need to fret on how the world's going,
if pure of the heart and God you are knowing.

Whatever your colour religion or creed,
hear words of Angels take warning and heed.
Don't stand in a panic obeying like sheep,
make certain with faith from temptation you keep.

Take just a moment to lift up your head,
total compliance to orders means dead.
God gives us instincts for knowing what's wrong,
so trust to your sense and don't follow along.

From very first moments from first early words,
they try to convince you that faith is absurd.
To me it seems simple there's one thing they fear,
believe in Lord Jesus keep uncensored thoughts clear.

41. Sky above.

The sky above once clear and blue,
trails of white cross over and through.
No natural cloud on haze of horizon,
the stubborn denial of what you lay eyes on.

Remember the days of childhood glee,
skies up above all chemical free.
Autism, dementia, indeed were still there,
few far between and praise the Lord rare.

Cancer we know causes death and deep hurting,
cures are all known but hid that is certain.
Honey bees dwindle for false given reasons,
nature's selection lie men with their treasons.

Pesticides chemicals and lab vaccinations,
destroying fertility in sweep across nations.
High up above sits milky white haze,
no more blue skies of childhood past days.

Can barely remember and not sure if true,
was the sky up above ever clear and just blue.
Mothers earth's dying see how she suffers,
destroy this one world and there aren't any others.

Conspiracy theories there always will be,
water so poisoned no fish in the sea.
Radiations slow leak watch oceans all die,
the Devils in power so crafty and sly.

Sean Michael McCarthy

Lift heads of awareness shout loud and raise voice,
start the protests whilst still chance of the choice.
Silent compliance upon which they rely,
all elite stood in power they think you won't try.

Installing false flags of terrorist fear,
pretend come to rescue and safely you steer.
Your freedom once sacred and fought for in wars,
slow strip away by sneak passing of laws.

The sky up above once clear and blue,
is God given right and given freely to you.
Demand that you get a summer and spring,
stop money worships they mean not a thing.

The sun it should shine and free rain must fall,
as nature intended not business's call.
Geo-engineering and climate control,
weapons of murder so massive the toll.

So sad to see that many don't care,
they see nothing wrong with white lines in the air.
Too late will it be when plans reach fruition,
initiative lost took too long to listen.

Ailments and illness and flooding then drought,
earthquakes and wars means profits about.
Sit alone in your darkness ask God what to do,
the sky up above once clear and blue.

42. Long lost friend

Remember me your long lost friend,
forgotten text on phone to send.
Money borrowed gone and spent,
absent mind to you I lent.

Free lifts home when you were stranded,
in pouring rain a queue jump handed.
Welcome smile and cheering word,
months that pass since I last heard.

It's always been that I am here,
for trouble sadness woe or fear.
When shoulder needed for you to lean,
for friendship then you're sudden keen.

Good old me with my advice,
always helpful always nice.
Time has come fair-weather friends,
to tell you all today it ends.

A new life calls me far away,
nothing left for me to say.
Time has come to put me first,
leave behind the past that's cursed.

Escape the place that drags me down,
leave behind sad seaside town.
Next time you search I won't be there,
lost confusion your empty stare.

Sean Michael McCarthy

Changed my number swapped my phone,
the old address no longer home.
Remember me your long lost friend,
reply to text you never send.

Only needed when times are bad,
somewhere to run when feeling sad.
A light in darkness when can't go on,
missed too late now I have gone.

Farewell to all the part time friend,
all good things in time must end.
Used abused then parting shove,
emotions bribe of friends should love.

No longer sucker to that deal,
empty words that you don't feel.
Been there done that t-shirt worn,
time to break all vows once sworn.

New life starts so old must end,
broken bridges too tired to mend.
The best thing left for all to do,
is walk away and start out new.

Memory fades the distant horizon,
on my back I feel your eyes on.
Hand to phone in hastened text,
I know the words that you'll send next.

Come back I need you please don't go,
did I say I love you so.
I need you want you here with me,
you can't escape you can't break free.

Too late for that this ship has sailed,
message returned delivery failed.
My number changed it is the end,
remember me your long lost friend.

43. Sitting on my bedroom floor.

Wish those days did longer last

My heart it slowed and nearly stopped,
with that bombshell that you dropped.
Hiding tears wiped into sleeve,
when you told me that you would leave.

Sitting on my bedroom floor,
with my back against the door.
Away you travelled half the world,
hugging knees you left me curled.

Time to start a whole new life,
farewell hurts cut deep like knife.
Numb with shock and full of pain,
knowing life won't be the same.

Left alone all by myself,
stripped of my most precious wealth.
Sitting on my bedroom floor,
with my back against the door.

Eyes all misty tears to wipe,
compose myself before we Skype.
Smile hello and give a wave,
put on act and face of brave.

So far apart so many miles,
eyes that sparkle tears of smiles.
Kept apart like sun and moon,
how I long to hug you soon.

A rush of words from me to you,
stories of adventures new.
New friends made new place to live,
who shall I my hugs now give.

Sitting on my bedroom floor,
with my back against the door.
I remember when your hair first curled,
for oh so long you've been my world.

First steps taken without my hand,
baby words to understand.
I'd rock you gently on just one arm,
a Fathers role to protect from harm.

Smiling down to meet your gaze,
you truly did my soul amaze.
Sitting on my bedroom floor,
with my back against the door.

Where's time gone so very fast,
wish those days did longer last.
Things like riding your first bike,
choosing comics you did like.

So many moments that I hold dear,
too long the list for you to hear.
My love for Ashlee, Maddie, Ben,
as strong today as was back then.

You filled my life with all things good,
I tried to do the best I could.
I hope that I got most things right,
and my hugs felt loving tight.

Every chance I'll shout out loud,
how you 3 all make me proud.
I know that some days I may feel sad,
just missing you is daft old dad.

To help to ease the loss I'm feeling,
I hang your pictures from floor to ceiling.
Sitting on my bedroom floor,
with my back against the door.

We have long chats via Skype on-line,
that cheer me almost every time.
It's late for you I see you yawning,
time zones make your night my morning.

Farewell with love and we'll speak soon,
once more alone inside my room.
Not feeling sad not now no more,
sitting on my bedroom floor.

44. World so wide.

half the world keeps us apart

No sadness can compare,
to children no longer there.
Not standing by my side,
parted by world so wide.

Your laugh and smile and voice,
so far by fate not choice.
How now my conscience tugs,
was I too mean with my hugs.

Too busy or always working,
quality time that I was shirking.
No sadness and free of fear,
if only I had you near.

Half the world keeps us apart,
ever constant in my heart.
Leaves me often feeling sad,
I'm not with you as your Dad.

Give you lifts or lend you money,
sharing laughs at things found funny.
At pictures as girl did pass,
Ashlee shouts out oh that ass.

Followed by hour long giggle fit,
thought girl about her meant it.
It was a dancer on the screen,
who's ass had Ashlee seen.

Remember Christmas day surprise,
could not believe my ears or eyes.
Maddison sings a song she wrote,
plays guitar to perfect note.

Oh how my eyes went wide,
and filled my heart with pride.
No sadness to my mind,
when such memories I can find.

Just love and feeling proud,
lifting spirits as high as cloud.
How can I ever feel real sad,
when you say we love you Dad.

Your pictures hang on wall,
perfect moments caught them all.
I love it when we Skype,
Ben waves his arms with hype.

It sometimes makes hurt worse,
this distance is a curse.
Heavy heart and longing sigh,
look to heaven asking why.

My Ash my Mad my Ben,
when will we hug again.
I long to see the day,
you come visit for a stay.

Parted by a world so wide,
when you left some tears I cried.
But soon the day will come,
together we'll have some fun.

Until that day I type,
Face book message or on Skype.
With all this love inside,
the world don't seem so wide.

45. Angels took your hand.

We find it hard to understand,
why Angels came to take your hand.
Took you from the ones you love,
led you to the skies above.

Your time was short and all too brief,
with endings comes such hurt and grief.
We had some laughs and lots of fun,
all came to end when just begun.

You need to know and need to see,
what losing you has meant to me.
Throughout my soul engraved in heart,
my love for you will never part.

I'll not feel sad I'll oust the glum,
no regrets on all stood done.
Moments of laughter and many the smile,
will dwell inside memory forever the while.

Always close and always near,
time of our life held cherished dear.
God's Angels came to take your hand,
took you to that promised land.

Left us behind with questions why,
hearts that sigh from no reply.
Not one regret in all we done,
life of laughs and lots of fun.

Not really gone just left the stage,
we'll re-unite in a future age.
Time will pass and slowly heal,
the loss and pain that we all feel.

You leave behind in memory,
the love you gave out all for free.
It helps us all to understand,
why Angels came to take your hand.

46. Christmas time.

Once again it's that time of year,
we're all supposed to feel good cheer.
But if you've sadly lost someone,
then Christmas time is not much fun.

It brings to mind that person dear,
taken away no longer here.
We never dreamed it would come to be,
so soon your absence from under the tree.

Paper hats at the big feast table,
give the gift with forgot price label.
Lost in thoughts of deep memory,
sits empty the chair where you really should be.

Everyone sharing all Christmas chores,
empty old slippers on bedroom floors.
Celebrations have all lost their edge,
unwanted reminders to up memory dredge.

Crackers get pulled the fake laughing fun,
jokes are so awful each every one.
Christmas traditions we all love to do,
just not the same when done without you.

Festive the season but just not the same,
no giving of gifts baring your name.
Stockings and puddings rich brandy taste,
Christmas time spirits all gone to waste.

Once again it's that time of year,
we're all supposed to feel good cheer.
Open so quick all gifts that were bought,
Face holding mask to hide the sad thought.

If people you know have lost a someone,
Father or Mother, Daughter or Son.
Maybe they smile and offer good cheer,
whilst deep down inside missing loved one not here.

All gifts without doubt they would willingly give,
for just 10 Christmas minutes once more to be with.
So as all of us sit around the big tree,
laughing with friends and all family.

Think of that someone that each of us know,
who tries very hard to not let pain show.
Give them some love and pass on good cheer,
they need it most this time of year.

47. Head under hood.

With head under hood and face hidden by mask,
violent destruction your soul aim and task.
In the slums of the world children sift through the litter,
lacking the food to make healthy and fitter.

You hang in a pack no courage alone,
film all your horrors on your mobile phone.
Mindless, immoral, you smash and you loot,
shopkeepers glass window put through with your boot.

You think you have life so harsh and unfair,
when many in world have nothing but air.
When you have thirst just turn on a tap,
children so needy from mud puddles must lap.

If hungry no problem just pop to the store,
kids die of hunger they starve wanting more.
You laugh and jig dance as you wreck and ruin,
look in the mirror think what you are doing.

Joe public works hard he scrimps and he saves,
what gives you the right to rock boat making waves.
John Doe loses work earns family no money,
his van that you torched cos you thought it was funny.

With head under hood and face hidden by mask,
what are your reasons for riot we ask.
Wearing posh clothes and designer made shoes,
behaving like heathens all over the news.

You show no respect no morals or soul,
violent aggression from booze from your dole.
The rich just get richer is one of your chants,
as you start burning houses in your Armani pants.

The sneakers you wear would cost a week's wages,
no reasons found valid for your ranting rages.
You don't have a job contribute no tax,
live off the state your endeavour it lacks.

You think life is hard on Great Britain streets,
look too the countries where true hardship beats.
You believe its fair game to steal from the old,
whilst hung around your necks thick silver and gold.

Syria, Palestine, Libya and Iraq,
here are people whose lives truly lack.
Do they smash burn and loot their own people and town,
or fight for the freedom from dictatorship Crown.

You pull up the paving to shop window smash,
bitter resentment when spent all your cash.
Do you fight for survival or clean drinking water,
do snipers and landmines kill sons or a daughter.

You riot through boredom envy and greed,
steal for the thrill not survival the need.
The Police you deem useless they stand looking on,
unable to act with mob thousands strong.

No water canon or bullets of rubber,
against human rights the weak minded blubber.
With head under hood and face hidden by mask,
you laugh your bravado left free at your task.

In days yet to come a Policeman will call,
for every street corner the camera saw all.
You'll scream like a baby as you get arrested,
see the stupidity of system thought bested.

The public and people whose lives you did ruin,
want justice seen done for the things you were doing.
No soft sentence given door slammed with a bang,
bring back the flogging and start a chain gang.

A cell with a bucket and mattress of straw,
this makes you truly see what is poor.
This country that strives for rights of the free,
if you don't like it then fuck off and flee.

How dare you run riot in city and town,
whilst all through the world children fall down.
Soldier's long dead all turn in the grave,
sad spirits stood witness your shameful behave.

When you look in a mirror I hope you feel shame,
the violent destruction was no x-box game.
People got hurt their whole lives destroyed,
no place left to work no longer employed.

You're mindless pathetic of this there's no doubt,
booze fuelled your actions like mindless drop out.
Once you leave prison you'll wish that you could,
walk down the street without head under hood.

48. Mums and Dads.

Mother or Mum is just one single word,
for all of our lives most of us heard.
Father or Dad is likewise another,
usually there to protect us from bother.

Comfort and hugs with tears dried by kisses,
squirming with blushes and stop it please wishes.
But once lost to heaven a Mum or a Dad,
we remember with longing those kisses we had.

The times we were injured with scrapes to the knee,
the scream of your name to come home for tea.
Sat at the table for big Sunday dinner,
with mountain sized portions pull wish bone a winner.

Mummy the normal uttered first word,
the delight on her face when finally heard.
Dad would spend hours day after day,
trying for Daddy your first word to say.

Don't tell your Father whispers your Mum,
our secret from Mummy winks Daddy your chum.
Both try to claim you as best ever friend,
always will love you right to the end.

Knees to the floor arms held out wide,
words to encourage first tottering stride.
Hands that will catch whenever you fall,
love that will answer if ever you call.

Sean Michael McCarthy

Our Mums and Dads they make and shape life,
ease all our worries and sort out the strife.
No single thought given that one day they'll leave,
their love given freely like the air that we breathe.

First failed romance with hearts feeling broke,
Mum buys us chocolate and Dad cracks a joke.
They pick us up gently put back on our feet,
tell us fish plenty in seas yet to meet.

When rocky paths seemed too scary or bleak,
with guidance and wisdom wise words they would speak.
A Mum and a Dad of each we have one,
both do their best to fill lives with fun.

When one has departed climbed stairs to Gods gate,
we cry out our anguish and wishes they'd wait.
It's hard to believe their time came to go,
left one behind to fly life solo.

They've always been there our sanity rock,
how could the Angels call time on their clock.
Gone from our vision like tears that we cried,
now deep inside hearts the memories hide.

Our first wobbly bike ride with Dad holding the seat,
running beside us helped accomplish this feat.
First day of school so certain we'd hate,
come 4 o'clock they'd wait by the gate.

The moment will come that none can avoid,
when loss drags a screaming heart to the void.
Try not to worry and don't you despair,
for once they have left a new Angel is there.

You are crowning glory and proof of their life,
the greatest achievement of Husband and Wife.
Mother or Mum and Father or Dad,
rejoice up with Angels for you that they had.

They remember the babies they cradled in arms,
stuck to their duty to protect from all harms.
Filled you with laughter compassion and love,
reaping rewards of the view from above.

They stand next to Jesus up high on a cloud,
see how they smile with hearts full and proud.
The loss brings deep pain in time that will fade,
left with all memories of fun times they made.

Think fondly of moments they smothered in love,
this magic gives wings to Angels above.
Soon Mummy and Daddy are words that are yours,
you comfort the tears, knee scrapes and sores.

The cycle continues it never does end,
your very own children to make your best friend.
Fill life full of wonder, laughter and love,
make Mummy and Daddy smile up above.

49. Innocent play.

Maddison sits in a box and she reads

I remember it all,
like just yesterday.
How you skipped and laughed,
in your innocent play.

My feelings of joy,
at my perfect heaven.
When you were all little,
aged 3, 5 and 7.

Ashlee who danced,
with a ballerina grace.
Maddison leading,
and setting the pace.

Ben sat in silence,
watches and stares.
Does somersaults,
backwards down stairs.

Maddison sits,
in a box as she reads.
Ben with his food,
cookie monster greed's.

Ashlee so full,
of compassion and love.
Before herself always,
puts others above.

Long summer walks,
on Woolacombe beach.
Skipping back laughing,
from wave foamy reach.

Walking together,
our footprints in sand.
Pretending adventures,
of Pirates on land.

Digging for shells,
and long lost gold treasure.
Those long summer days,
of fun at our leisure.

Memories we have,
of magic times past.
Remembered forever,
for always to last.

I look back with wonder,
engraved in my mind.
The moments of magic,
so plenty to find.

First day of school,
Ashlee was worried.
At home time excited,
her stories she hurried.

Maddison so clever,
a prolific quick reader.
Ben just as always,
the same greedy feeder.

My children so different,
like sunshine and rain.
If perfection the goal,
then I win the game.

Together forever,
2 sisters and brother.
Each is unique,
unlike any other.

They fill me with love,
and joy of great pride.
Never alone,
with these memories inside.

Too soon did you grow,
too busy to play.
I remember it all,
like just yesterday.

Trips to the pictures,
and Walt Disney movie.
When hanging with dad,
was cool and still groovy.

Remember the days,
we use to go bowling.
Ben used the shoot,
to start his ball rolling.

How fast that he wanted,
to hurry his turn.
For food on the table,
his interest would yearn.

Day trips of adventure,
to wild life park.
Cousin Sheryden along,
to join in the lark.

Remember the trip,
to Cleethorpes near Grimsby.
Our upgrade to 5 start,
got given for free.

We went to the fair,
and on roller you'd coast.
Ben got so scared,
on that train with the ghost.

On that big tower,
straight up you flew.
Screams came from Ashlee,
as she lost a shoe.

The big games of golf,
on courses so crazy.
Ben kept on moaning,
'cos tired hungry and lazy.

Some memories so precious,
diamonds coated in gold.
Forever my heart,
will these moments hold.

On Christmas mornings,
I'd try not to wake.
As into your bedrooms,
full stockings I'd take.

They'd be full of chocolates,
and Smurfs small and blue.
Books games and pencils,
some bubble bath too.

All sat in pyjamas,
around Christmas tree.
Handing out prezzies,
this big one's from me.

The box was shaped funny,
what is it you say.
Frantic unwrapping,
a guitar to now play.

A gift from cat Topsy,
and one from Baloo.
And here's one from Santa,
left here for you.

The fun times of Birthdays,
with video take.
We all sung the song,
blow out candles on cake.

Sean Michael McCarthy

I remember it all,
like just yesterday.
You skipped and laughed,
in your innocent play.

Saturday mornings,
we'd head to the pool.
Fun hour frolics,
like an acrobat fool.

Ben would rush in,
to grab a blue mat.
Wouldn't be happy,
if he couldn't do that.

All squashed together,
in our pretend boat.
Me shouting earthquake,
as i shook the float.

After each swim,
came the vending machine.
Chocolates and sweets,
for this Ben was keen.

Remember the day,
that you learnt to ride.
Your first 2 wheel bike,
as I ran beside.

Ashlee who wobbled,
her balance unsure.
Maddison not once,
put feet to the floor.

Down in the car park,
by Hillsboro Hill.
You girls were so happy,
you thought it was brill'.

A day at the beach,
I taught you to fish.
Ben didn't like,
how the seaweed went squish.

Of course we caught nothing,
not one single bite.
So off to the chip shop,
for our tea that night.

Our house on the hill,
old number 18.
Just think of the memories,
that old place has seen.

It wasn't massive,
at the same time not small.
But perfectly just right,
and home for us all.

We had us a cat,
and a dog called Baloo.
Who licked at Ben's bum,
when he'd just done a poo.

Fish birds and rabbits,
and a hamster or three.
Sure filled our house,
with fun times and glee.

Remember when Ben,
was hiding aloof.
Found up in loft,
throwing videos on roof.

And dear little Maddy,
Easter eggs hide and hog.
I'd sneak in and eat them,
and then blame the dog.

You tried roller skating,
down Cambridge Grove.
Down the hill so easy,
then back up you strove.

A pool in the garden,
and a big trampoline.
Sometimes a big frog,
behind shed would be seen.

So many moments,
sit frozen in time.
All happy memories,
3 Amigo's of mine.

I remember them all,
like just yesterday.
You skipped and laughed,
in your innocent play.

50. My Angela.

Never again is what I swore,
bury the key to my hearts door.
Too hard for me to once more trust,
or flames of passion my heart thrust.

To take the risk on one more chance,
feel the butterflies in stomach dance.
You gave a smile just for me,
no strings attached it was for free.

I've been so hurt I'm damaged goods,
my life of wander lost in woods.
Still you reached to take my hand,
head held high beside me stand.

Can it be I've finally found,
a soul mate to my heart astound.
In you my trust I place complete,
to do so is no easy feat.

I want it yes but I'm still wary,
to risk more hurt is somewhat scary.
When our eyes meet my worries melt,
a warming feel inside is felt.

I'll give you all that's mine to give,
for ever and each day I live.
I'll be your soul mate lover friend,
to all your needs I swear to tend.

When words are sometimes hard to find,
I'll write you poems and songs that rhymed.
But you flowers just you see,
give you hugs and kiss for free.

Sometimes words they just won't do,
for saying things like I love you.
So here I write for all to see,
my Angela means the world to me.

51. Sparkle in my eye.

You are the smile upon my lips,
the sparkle in my eye.
You are the spring in my step,
my searched for reason why.

You are the beat within my heart,
the rhythm of my soul.
You are the game of my life,
my scoring winning goal.

You are my jigsaws final piece,
you make my life complete.
You are an Angel from the heavens,
sent down for me to meet.

You are my Karma, fate and fortune,
my longed for destiny.
Our souls have travelled many miles,
and searched for century.

And now we are at last together,
it's not the journeys end.
We are adventures just begun,
my soul mate lover friend.

You are my light along the path,
of wonder, love and awe.
You are the holder of the key,
that opened my hearts door.

You are the magic in my world,
the fulfilment of my life.
You are the granting of my wish,
to have you as my wife.

You are the one that's always there,
forever standing by.
You are the smile upon my lips,
the sparkle in my eye.

52. Remember.

Remember the days when summers were long,
clear blue skies full of bird song.
Remember at school the halls full of hymn,
grab seat at the back if first to get in.

Remember that bottle of milk on first break,
ensuring nutrition each day we would take.
Remember we'd yearn for lunch break the most,
huge games of football with school jumper post.

Remember that school tin full of pencils and pen,
watching the Wombles and Mr Men.
Remember when school days stopped at half 4,
running home fast no key for latched door.

Remember Mum asking if you had some homework,
dry the days dishes a chore wished to shirk.
Remember the shout to come home for tea,
swinging like Tarzan from branches in tree.

Remember the games kiss chase hide and seek,
by sending love letters young couples would speak.
Remember T.V. on a Saturday morning,
Swap shop, The Monkeys such fun never boring.

Remember the pictures called afternoon flicks,
playing at Zoro with swords made from sticks.
Remember on Sundays the big family dinner,
all races you ran you finished as winner.

Remember the joy of climbing a tree,
like Everest conquered with scrape to the knee.
Remember that first bike a chopper so red,
no bell for ringing a honk horn instead.

Remember the games Mouse-trap Kerplunk,
games that today kids would deem junk.
Remember the church bell and Sunday school fun,
fast as you can for ice-cream van run.

Remember the days the lists full of chores,
get them all done and pocket money is yours.
Remember the days of long summer sun,
care free and easy and so full of fun.

Remember the test match of single stump cricket,
games got abandoned lost ball in a thicket.
Remember you thought most things were strife,
ignored mothers wisdom best days of your life.

Remember the milkman driving his float,
if needing some extra you'd just leave a note.
Remember the sweet shop and 4 for a penny,
these days a whole pound doesn't buy many.

Remember when winning the great games with marble,
comics called Beano, Dandy and Marvel.
Remember adventures we've done and seen,
for as you get older it's a favourite dream.

Remember the days you could run and not ache,
Monopoly, Scrabble, played on picnics you'd take.
Remember that Christmas delight at your hoard,
when Santa delivered the longed for skate board.

Remember when asking for puppy or kitten,
for 3 or 4 weeks being totally smitten.
Remember the magic holding first lovers warm hand,
the excitement and wonder as first kiss did land.

Remember the games played by us all,
the kicking of cans or thrown tag tennis ball.
Remember the summers of fun in the park,
out riding bikes from dawn until dark.

Remember by torchlight whilst duvet hid under,
reading of books such adventure and wonder.
Remember when Gran would sit and sip tea,
sneak you the fortune of a whole 50p.

Remember believing in Easters old bunny,
teeth under pillow for tooth fairy money.
Remember the love in Mothers warm hug,
Dad ruffles hair with back pat and a shrug.

Remember the fights with Sister or Brother,
and if you lost the run to tell Mother.
Remember the wonder of space man and moon.
how we were certain we'd be living there soon.

Remember for breakfast soldiers of toast,
with 2 boiled eggs we'd like that the most.
Remember your youth as the years make you old,
moments long gone more precious than gold.

Remember when children we'd never grow old,
best days of life we always were told.
Remember the days when summers were long,
clear blue skies full of bird song.

53. Taken.

Taken by Angels taken too soon,
taken to heaven past the stars and the moon.
Taken from family taken from friends,
taken from loved ones what means to such ends.

Taken from memory taken from dream,
taken from hearts all you have been.
Taken from tears the drops that we cry,
taken from sadness your spirit to fly.

Taken to glory taken too young,
taken to paradise where your name is sung.
Taken from us taken from view,
taken from life now God cradles you.

54. Inspiration flutters by.

Inspiration flutters by,
riding waves of tears we cry.
Life slips so quick to cruel from kind,
no words of comfort can we find.

Hearts that burst with heavy sigh,
look to heaven ask God why.
The love we feel does forever bind,
all moments shared that fill our mind.

We search for answers to questions why,
the Angels took you up to the sky.
No reasons good can we find,
to masters plan we all stand blind.

Left us behind with tears to dry,
staring up as clouds float by.
With thoughts of you all hearts are lined,
full memory book you shared and signed.

You sparkle now a star up high,
and float on breeze like butterfly.
Your whispered words they ruffle hair,
a gentle wind is that you there.

Along the path of light you find,
heavens gates are Angel lined.
You moved on with a peaceful sigh,
you're inspiration fluttered by.

55. Dear Daddy.

We know you must leave us, the time come to part.
But for always dear Daddy, you'll live in my heart.
The words that we offer, can't mend the pain.
From this day forever, life just not the same.

Gone from my side, taken too soon.
Angels in heaven, lead you from the room.
Tears from the heart, that slide from my eye.
Time spent together, how quick it did fly.

Magical moments, we shared through the years.
Remember us laughing, so hard it brought tears.
Always beside me, you catch every fall.
You came to my rescue, at every first call.

Some call him father, most just use Dad.
When Angels come take them, we miss what we had.
Distant past memories, now cloud our eyes.
Looking to heaven, with Oh Daddy cries.

All seems surreal, a bad dream not true.
Eyes closed so tightly, just wishing for you.
Daddy you've left us, stepped out from this life.
Angels came took you, away from all strife.

They saw how you suffer, could take it no more.
They opened their wings, you to heaven their chore.
Adventures we've taken, and the memories made.
Very first bike ride, beside me you stayed.

Always there with me, strength by my side.
Through all my hardships, loved me with pride.
Oh how I miss you, now that you went.
Could we have better, our last moments spent.

Did I tell you I love you, could you see it was true.
My hero my rock, by just being you.
Don't linger in sadness, you walk to that light.
As family and friends, will see I'm alright.

We'll gather in sadness, and share many tears.
We'll remember the magic, you gave us for years.
You leave us all broken, but still standing strong.
You taught us such wonders, as life went along.

Now Daddy keep moving, don't you be late.
Climb all those white steps, right up to the gate.
Clouds lined with Angels, all waiting it's true.
Each their in person, to welcome you.

We know you must leave us, the time come to part.
But for always dear Daddy, you'll live in my heart.
The ghost of your memory will carry me through,
Forever together our love will stand true.

56. We know someone.

We know someone that is no more,
they left their soul outside the door.
Quit the race and left the room,
memories swept away too soon.

Tired of struggle worn down by woe,
made the choice to up and go.
What's the point of struggle on,
if not one person will notice gone.

Never speak or never call,
adds more bricks to defensive wall.
World spins by in frantic pace,
stands like statue in the race.

We know someone that is no more,
different from us the judgement poor.
Hardly seen and rarely heard,
soon extinct like Dodo bird.

Out of sight and absent from mind,
deemed to be a boring kind.
Avoids all limelight spirits sink,
read your eyes knows what you think.

Materialistic that most adore,
all the focus on owning more.
A persons wealth when comes the end,
measured at grave by numbers of friend.

If standing alone the choice they make,
then better that than friendship fake.
Who are you to try to sway,
if they choose to shun your way.

Life for living yes indeed,
each must choose just what they need.
Some say opposites can attract,
challenge to change may be the fact.

Grind them down wear them out,
is this what life is all about.
Don't you think can't you see,
they're quite content just to be.

We know someone that is no more,
memory lost in archives store.
Once their shadow shared our path,
gone the moments that prompted laugh.

Left behind by life of fast pace,
strive to lead the rats in race.
Father Brother Uncle Son,
Sister Aunty Daughter Mum.

If they choose to stand and stare,
doesn't mean they no longer care.
Time still moves upon the clock,
stepping back and taking stock.

Re-assess the life to lead,
prioritize the things to need.
How many notice the empty space,
failed recognition of the face.

Out of sight and out of mind,
with a shrug the new friend find.
You shut them out and lock the door,
and know someone that is no more.

57. I'm still the same.

I'm still the same,
why can't you see.
Don't turn away,
abandon me.

Lost my wings,
can no longer fly.
I won't give up,
I can but try.

I've sat with you,
around the tree.
To watch your eyes,
fill with Christmas glee.

I've sang along,
with Birthday cheers.
Smiling through,
those happy tears.

I'm still the same,
why can't you see.
You mean the world,
in whole to me.

Lost my wings,
can no longer soar.
Still I'll battle,
take on the chore.

I've held you close,
when you were sad.
Stood by your side,
when things went bad.

I've picked you up,
each time you fell.
And dragged you back,
from depressions hell.

I'm still the same,
why can't you see.
Now standing strong,
no lean on me.

Lost my wings,
can no longer glide.
But still I walk,
with you beside.

I held your hand,
when you were scared.
I listened deep,
to your soul bared.

I took you in,
when all doors shut.
No questions why,
no ifs or but.

I'm still the same,
why can't you see.
Without a you,
there is no me.

Lost my wings,
can no longer fly.
Lost from heaven,
can't reach the sky.

I've dried your tears,
when you were low.
Fought your corner,
through friend and foe.

I took your heart,
exchanged with mine.
I promised you,
all was fine.

I'm still the same,
why can't you see.
Broke down your walls,
I set you free.

I lost my wings,
can no longer claim.
Heavens blessings,
or an Angels fame.

Am I want,
or was I need.
Where do I stand,
now you are freed.

Gone are hugs,
no laughs or fun.
Distant dreams,
of things once done.

Don't like the rules,
of this game.
Why can't you see,
I'm still the same.

58. Forgotten.

Sometimes I feel forgotten,
like a shadow with no sun.
I stand alone in corners,
whilst you party and you fun.

I see the looks and glances,
and hear your whispered words.
My thoughts are out the window,
flying free with all the birds.

I've severed all connections,
from the rats still in the race.
A façade of deep reflection,
the mask across my face.

Silence screams the loudest,
in a world on volume full.
To follow all the masses,
resist that urgent pull.

Sometimes I feel forgotten,
like a shadow in the shade.
Slipped right out of memory,
the moment hardly stayed.

Past ties they've slowly faded,
like wisps of smoke on wind.
Those no longer needy,
how quick your friendship binned.

I can count them now with fingers,
and only use one hand.
Those I see as comrades,
by side of me still stand.

The names still go with faces,
on people I once knew.
Their paths go different places,
false friendships now seen through.

Sometimes I feel forgotten,
like a shadow in the night.
Merge into the corners,
hide away from all limelight.

Standing there not noticed,
a skill that few achieve.
Watching all the motions,
of the webs that people weave.

Falsehoods fakes and liars,
the world of dog eat dog.
The strive for more possession,
an up-hill battle slog.

Is it any wonder,
that I strive to break the rules.
Step away from the it crowd,
with your antics fit for fools.

Sometimes I feel forgotten,
like a shadow of myself.
Once known but now forgotten,
abandoned on dust strewn shelf.

Too tired to make the effort,
and old to change my way.
I blend into the background,
people watching my whole day.

Do you ever wonder,
how friendships fade away.
Like shadows merge to darkness,
at end of sunshine day.

Some will think me loner,
a man without a friend.
Sometimes I feel forgotten,
that's it that's all the end.

59. A piece of me.

Left me memories forever stay

Ever since you moved away,
a piece of me dies each day.
To not have children close or near,
a parents hearts greatest fear.

Often words are hard to find,
how close the bonds that tie and bind.
Not 'til lost do we see,
how much a hug can mean to me.

Who has to travel 9,000 miles,
just to see their children's smiles.
That's the deal no other choice,
to hear in person their laughing voice.

Ever since you moved away,
I miss you more and more each day.
New adventures you can explore,
who indeed could ask for more.

Are you happy are you glad,
cope without long distant Dad.
Opportunities that set you free,
make me smile feel happy.

Make new friends a whole new life,
escape from England and it's strife.
Exciting journeys world so wide,
fills your old Dad up with pride.

Ever since you moved away,
left me memories forever stay.
Sometimes i sit alone and stare,
then realise no longer there.

No longer close or by my side,
separated by world so wide.
To feel alone and somewhat lost,
heavy price that is the cost.

It is the burden that I must bare,
your happiness my one true care.
But since you left I cannot lie,
a piece of me each day will die.

60. Summer came.

Summer came and then it went,
too few the days in sunshine spent.
Far between and quick to pass,
of running barefoot on the grass.

The skies start clear quick to cloud,
mood smothered like reapers shroud.
Remember how we use to see,
the bumbling of that buzzing bee.

And picnics when we use to fear,
flight path of wasp that comes too near.
Chase by friends through fields of corn,
games of cricket on carpet lawn.

Summer came and then it went,
seaside trips with postcards sent.
Clothes discarded paddle wade,
wishing that we longer stayed.

Up with birds at early lark,
grand adventure to fun theme park.
Days stretched long and full of sun,
plenty the light to get things done.

If whole day spent on things to do,
evening reward of bar-be-queue.
Holidays we took abroad,
exotic berths of ships we board.

Summer came and then it went,
ladies holding hands of Gent.
Smile content of love they made,
whilst evening stroll on promenade.

Life so good and feeling fine,
if sun will only always shine.
But evenings darken all too soon,
fill the skies with star and moon.

Even this would be no pain,
so long as stays away the rain.
Just eight long months we must survive,
before summer can again arrive.

Sean Michael McCarthy

61. Follow your dreams.

Follow your dreams,
follow your heart.
Right to the end,
as soon as you start.

Live for each moment,
days full of fun.
Happy contented,
when each day is done.

The world is your oyster,
the popular phrase.
Everything possible,
when love fills your days.

Some think it scary,
to step out on your own.
Leaving all loved ones,
behind at your home.

But where ever you travel,
whatever the land.
We're always beside you,
holding your hand.

You fill us with wonder,
and fill us with pride.
Everyone loves you,
the fact we can't hide.

Our Angels will guard you,
on the journeys you take.
Over high mountains,
or crystal clear lake.

Your life of adventure,
it's time to begin.
Whatever the challenge,
we know you will win.

The leaving of loved ones,
we know this is hard.
Just keep us happy,
via Skype or postcard.

62. 13 Years.

I can't believe it's been 13 years,
since you left and all the tears.
13 years have gone so fast,
on this day your shadow cast.

15th day of the month July,
memories pain makes all hearts cry.
I can't believe it's been 13 years,
since we raised our glass to wish you cheers.

13 years the time has flown,
look at us how old we've grown.
But not for you you're just the same,
up in heaven no strife or pain.

Brother Son Cousin Friend,
Angels that your heart now tend.
You live each day inside of me,
deep in soul and memory.

I can't believe it's been 13 years,
and still this day can bring some tears.
We miss your laugh and your smile,
you're cheeky japes and cunning guile.

You'd poke our ribs or flick our ear,
to announce to all RUMBO is here.
Infect the room with joyful fun,
light up the world like mornings sun.

I can't believe it's been 13 years,
that moment sad that a mother fears.
Lost to all on that road in Devon,
God's V.I.P. pass for you to heaven.

13 years in a blink of eye,
we still all struggle for the reason why.
Gone too soon we all agree,
from struggle of life you flew free.

Those left behind we all grow old,
memory of you in stories told.
We cry and laugh and shout out loud,
you smile whilst sat upon your cloud.

Today's the day 15th July,
remember you with heart heavy sigh.
RUMBO is listening be certain he hears,
I can't believe it's been 13 years.

63. The Angels came.

The Angels came, stole you away,
how easy you, their words did sway.
The sweetest music, you ever heard,
whispered "come with us", the magic word.

We'll take you up, above the stars,
and love you dearly, when you're ours.
Stop all the pain, and ease your woe,
come take our hand, and let us go.

The Angels came, stole you away,
too good for earth, for you to stay.
They want to see, your smiling face,
bathed in the glory, of heavens grace.

They deemed you'd struggled, on too long,
lift up thy voice, to heavens song.
They stand around you, and implore,
come take our hands, come explore.

We have such wonders, for you to see,
just say the word, we'll set you free.
The Angels came, stole you away,
could not leave you lost, another day.

They saw how hard, you struggled by,
moved to tears, you made them cry.
Like nightingale, that magic bird,
the call to heaven, is finally heard.

Oh pearly gates, on which you gaze,
stood before, do true amaze.
The clouds around, they are all full,
of Angels witness, to Gods pull.

Through to chimes, of bells that ring,
Avenues, of cherubs sing.
The Angles came, stole you away,
before the lord, you kneel today.

His gentle hand, upon your head,
today you're born, no longer dead.
He gives you robes, of purest white,
and cleanses soul, with heavens light.

Upon your back, he places wings,
oh my heaven, hear how it sings.
Just rewards, for life lived well,
though at the time, you couldn't tell.

Life spent giving, kindness love,
the secret key, to gates above.
Left to Angels, every choice,
they pick the ones, to hear their voice.

Magic whispered, for you to hear,
heart was lifted, free of fear.
Your eyes now closed, at peace you lay,
the Angels came, stole you away.

"The Angels Came" By Sean McCarthy Inspiration provided by Wesley
Norman 14/01/66 - 30/01/15

64. There comes a time.

There comes a time,
we all must share.
When we turn to find,
a friend not there.

They've left this world,
moved on by.
Gone chasing stars,
up in the sky.

Joined the throng,
at end of queue.
At pearly gates,
the slow walk through.

There comes a time,
that brings an end.
All hearts will ache,
from loss of friend.

The first to go,
and all too soon.
His life's new challenge,
to catch the moon.

Left on earth,
all pains and woe.
When Angels whispered,
it's time to go.

There comes a time,
that we all dread.
Each will hear,
their old pals dead.

Closed his eyes,
gave up the fight.
The long hard struggle,
used up his might.

We all have moments,
in memories dear.
That keep old Wesley,
forever near.

His crazy japes,
the things thought fun.
We'd shake our heads,
at things he done.

He'd jump off cliffs,
and land in pool.
Just 4ft deep,
the bloody fool.

He'd always care,
give helping hand.
If ever the need,
beside you stand.

Sean Michael McCarthy

There comes a time,
we all do fear.
Who will be first,
Grim Reapers sneer.

It's just like Wez,
to jump the queue.
I'll go first,
just let me through.

He had no fear,
or thought for himself.
Whenever flush,
he'd share his wealth.

He's left us now,
escaped from Devon.
Joined Angels gang,
up high in heaven.

We'll miss you mate,
and we'll hurt a while.
But in months to come,
you'll make us smile.

We'll remember back,
on times so fine.
Our hearts they know,
there comes a time.

"There comes a time" By Sean McCarthy 31/01/15 In memory of Wesley
Norman 14/01/66 - 30/01/15 Sleep well my old mate.

65. It's hard to believe.

It's hard to believe your time came to go,
years flashed by fast when time moved so slow.
Remember those days when we feared no danger,
the whole world ahead when aged as teenager.

We laughed and we joked in life free of fear,
never did dream the end could come near.
In blink of an eye the curtain can fall,
when Angels decide on who's name to call.

To most it's a number called forty-nine,
for you the Lord called out time.
It's hard to believe that someone still young,
from out of living so quickly gets flung.

Remember the nights full of laughter and japes,
leaving Sandpiper for Bunches or Grapes.
The races we ran up Mullacott Hill,
Stuart still finished despite being ill.

Nights down to Woolacombe at the long bar,
long dark walk home cos none had a car.
It's hard to believe your time came to leave,
such passion for life with heart on your sleeve.

Back in mid 80's down Speakeasy bar,
best misfits pool team in this town by far.
We played for the laughter the giggles and fun,
by end of the night we'd usually won.

Remember the races along the high street,
that lamppost collision knocked you off your feet.
After the disco things would get silly,
Tracey who dared you to mustard your willy.

So many moments of crazy filled days,
so long ago that memories haze.
It's hard to believe you're no longer here,
hearts that now miss you squeeze out a tear.

What are you doing up high on that cloud,
do you sit quietly or still laugh out loud.
Are you with old Gods playing bowls and some snooker,
or out with the Angels playing skittle and euchre.

Wesley my old mate see what you do,
even when left us we still think of you.
All through our lives you walked by our side,
always there with us matched stride for stride.

Gone from our life but still in our world,
often through mind your spirit is hurled.
Remember forever forgotten hell no,
it's hard to believe your time came to go.

66. Butterfly mornings.

Dawns bird chorus of love lullaby's,
rainbow reflections of your eyes.
Heavenly bliss of another day dawning,
peaceful dance of butterfly morning.

Such are the feelings of the world,
when babies new in arms are curled.
Little bundles pure bliss and joy,
Daddies little princess mums special boy.

Hearts that discover new depths of love,
such wonder admired by Angels above.
Life faded dull now so full of light,
everything perfect everything right.

Thanks to the heavens for sending the gift,
hearts so happy with high spirit lift.
Be it your 1st, 2nd or 3rd,
pride shouted out so whole world has heard.

Nothing comes close to the passion and joy,
as new baby arrival of girl or a boy.
As perfect as night sky star shining moon,
walks in a meadow wild flower afternoon.

Our own little Angels given new life,
Mummy and Daddy Husband and Wife.
They fill life with wonder passion and love,
sent down by Angels that watch from above.

Love them protect them forever yours,
be they perfect perfection or with some few flaws,
Butterfly mornings may they be with you soon.
enjoy each and every wild flower afternoon.

67. 32 Years.

32 years have come and past,
long time gone since hugged you last.
It only seems like yesterday,
that Angels came took you away.

Up beyond the moon and stars,
Heaven welcomed that mum of ours.
Left behind big empty space,
where sits the memory of your face.

Our hearts they sigh each every day,
since Angels came took you away.
Life back then was hard but fun,
you gave your love to each every one.

Spark of life inside your eyes,
you sang such love in lullabies.
32 years has quick flown by,
yet still the loss can make us cry.

We think of you day or night,
miss the way you hugged us tight.
Made us strong just and true,
qualities passed down from you.

Loss and sorrow the price we pay,
when Angel hands lead you away.
Still for you i cry my tears,
despite the passing of many years.

Left us behind with memory,
in God's kingdom now trouble free.
On the other side of Heaven's gate,
I know with hugs you patient wait.

The day will come we'll meet again,
in Angels care 'til comes that when.
Thanks dear mum for us you made,
our love for you will never fade.

Spirits and soul still love you true,
hearts hold dear memory of you.
32 years have come and past,
long time gone since hugged you last.

68. Granny Grimbles.

Granny Grimbles was her name,
grand size grumbles was her game.
If you didn't move really quick,
she's catch you with her naughty stick.

Loved by all down near the pier,
walk on down and bound to see her.
Sitting up on balcony,
let us in throw down the key.

Whenever walk with kids did take,
we'd pop on in for tea and cake.
Granny Grimbles was always fun,
beware the naughty she'd smack your bum.

She liked to laugh and maybe tease,
always thank you after please.
Of our family she was the head,
into mischief so easily led.

Today's the day that you were born,
no longer here feel not forlorn.
Live on forever inside our heart,
memories we have will never part.

Yes you may be now in heaven,
I bet your cloud is above your Devon.
You sit above us looking down,
watching all in your old town.

You see who's naughty or not good,
smack their bottoms if you could.
All that's left for us to say,
Granny Grimbles Happy Birthday.

69. Mummy dear.

Looking back on all we've done,
always close by stood our Mum.
Close at hand to banish fear,
ever ready to catch each tear.

Mummy was our first spoken word,
soft lullabies that we first heard.
Arms that held us safe at night,
we ran to her at every fright.

Guiding light along our paths,
we had some fun and lots of laughs.
If we tripped and fell down flat,
she always laughed hard when we did that.

But she'd come and still be there,
heart so full of love and care.
Life is hard when Mother's left,
hearts once whole now in two cleft.

Who can ease this pain today,
now that Angels took you away.
Oh Mummy dear i hope you see,
how all your love enriched me.

Filled with wonder from your smiles,
felt your love across the miles.
Always knowing that you were there,
as through old pictures I now stare.

Me aged seven sat on your knee,
moments caught so perfectly.
I'll miss you mum forever true,
sad that Angels came took you.

But in times of sadness or feeling glum,
looking back on all we've done.
My heart will swell and spirits lift,
from the love you gave as gift.

Goodbye dear Mummy you sleep well,
you've got your wings i heard that bell.
Up in heaven where you now rest,
that special place that takes the best.

70. 52, 52.

52,
52.
Today's the day,
we all think of you.

You haven't grown old,
you're still feeling great.
Sat on that cloud,
aged 38.

Taken from us,
up to the skies.
Left all behind,
with oh Rumbo cries.

Time is a healer,
it covers all pain.
Once we all wondered,
could life be the same.

The years pass by fast,
in blink of an eye.
Yet still just your memory,
brings tears to an eye.

52,
52.
I wonder what it is,
today that you do.

Sean Michael McCarthy

Do you lay dozing,
high on that cloud.
Are you out drinking,
is it allowed.

Are wings discarded,
whilst you have your fun.
Put back on tomorrow,
when the party is done.

With Angels as partners,
the japes you can pull.
With such adventures,
are our own memories full.

We're all getting older,
surpassing your years.
I bet up in heaven,
your laughter brings tears.

Oh cousin Rumbo,
we all still miss you.
Have the happiest birthday,
52, 52.

71. In coming years.

Remember me in coming years,
happy smiles and free of tears.
Lingered memories of all things done,
treasured moments each every one.

The time soon came for me to part,
game called over did barely start.
Life flashed by in blink of eye,
Angels lead my soul to sky.

Body tired breathes last sigh,
Heavens peace with wings to fly.
Leave the world and all that's glum,
barely noticed by things I've done.

Nothing special to you amaze,
no epic deeds to fill with praise.
Normal no-one working hard,
not one moment truly starred.

Did my shift and worked my time,
now in queue on heavens line.
If live life well is final test,
I did more good than most the rest.

Got things wrong yes often many,
for excuses I haven't any.
Just a normal plain old chap,
letting go of all life's crap.

Wipe your eyes and dry your tears,
where I go gives me no fears.
Moving on to somewhere nice,
with the Angels in paradise.

They witnessed life with all its deeds,
deemed me just what heaven needs.
So lift your glass and sing out cheers,
remember me in coming years.

72. These words now read.

If you hear these words now read,
it's come to pass that I am dead.
I've left you all to stand alone,
remove my number from your phone.

To see my name upon your screen,
will bring you tears and I'll feel mean.
Whilst up above in star filled skies,
I'll hear your hearts hurt anguish cries.

If you hear these words now read,
empty heart of woe and dread.
I closed my eyes and held them tight,
went on with Angels in the night.

They came to me inside a dream,
stood to witness all I have been.
They've seen me try and watched me fail,
and not give up to no avail.

I tried my best to choose the right,
for all things good I'd stand and fight.
There were mistakes I see it true,
but I did my best to stand by you.

All aches and pains melt away,
soothed by Angels hands today.
I float like ashes on a breeze,
slip from life with gentle ease.

If you hear these words now read,
understand how my path led.
Know that heaven welcomes me,
see how Angels set me free.

All I loved each everyone,
I tried to give in life some fun.
Sleep the sleep so longed for deep,
pass on my soul to Angels keep.

Permit me please if I'm allowed,
to sometimes sit on edge of cloud.
To look down upon all those below,
who cried some tears when I did go.

My watching eyes and wings kept hidden,
they won't see me for it's forbidden.
My memory ghost drifts through your head,
if you hear these words now read.

73. Time the great healer.

Time the great healer,
the words that we say.
When Angels from heaven,
steal a loved one away.

The passing of years,
in blink of an eye.
Long lonely moments,
of tears that we cry.

Hearts are still aching,
beating through pain.
Feelings of loss,
they still feel the same.

Long distant memories,
dance through our mind.
The reasons they chose you,
only Angels can find.

Did they see how we loved you,
do you think that they cared.
Did they stop and consider,
the love that we shared.

Time the great healer,
is often not true.
Every minute of moment,
we're still missing you.

The hurt and the sorrow,
our hearts full of pride.
Our very own Angel,
they stole from our side.

Each every morning,
we open our eyes.
Look to the heavens,
and search through the skies.

Are you up there above us,
do you hear our hearts sigh.
Every minute of moment,
inside us we cry.

Sometimes we awaken,
from dreams filled of you.
Is that magic from heaven,
sent us by from you.

Our sleep full of wonder,
of things could have been.
The world full of magic,
that you could have seen.

Time the great healer,
for some this is true.
Cloud the minds memory,
with new things to do.

But not one moment passes,
not one second of day.
That we wish that the Angels,
had left you to stay.

High up in heaven,
all free of pain.
To wash away tears,
you send down the rain.

To lift our low spirits,
a rainbow you'll send.
As Angels of heaven,
your heart now tend.

We walk on through life,
your memory inside.
Whilst shadows of Angels,
beside us they glide.

We carry you with us,
all the love that we feel.
The pain of love stolen,
time will not heal.

74. The day will come.

The day will come when we wake up dead,
all thoughts and worry drained from head.
No things to do and get all wrong,
no radio playing reminder song.

Body stiff and turning cold,
life flashed by of journey old.
Things we've done and places seen,
fade from world like misty dream.

Left the race and quit the game,
no feelings left to catch the pain.
It's no problem we don't mind,
left the world of cruel to kind.

Leave behind all hurt flung words,
soul flies free amongst the birds.
The day will come when we wake up dead,
regret those things you harshly said.

Those we love we target most,
left behind the memory ghost.
They tried their best to do things well,
yearned for words of praise to tell.

But words and love you gave was tough,
efforts fell short of good enough.
We find it easier to criticise,
too late the praise once someone dies.

Once departed passed through the gate,
words so loving arrive too late.
Remember how you puffed and panted,
negative feedbacks that you ranted.

The day will come when we wake up dead,
wish for kind words spoke instead.
Thanks for efforts and loving sigh,
ok not perfect but at least the try.

Life is hard no blueprint plan,
we try to do the best we can.
Sometimes right but often not,
done for you is what's forgot.

Left the world to sit up high,
float with Angels through the sky.
On fluffy clouds looking down,
shake of head and sadness frown.

Hear your moan and hear your grumble,
words that make all Angels tumble.
Listening to your complaining words said,
the day will come when we wake up dead.

75. She was.

She was my Grandma and your Mum,
our hearts flow over with memories done.
In quiet moments for 13 years,
hearts so heavy still squeeze out tears.

It sometimes seems like yesterday,
that Angels came took her away.
You held her hand and said goodbye,
cheeks that glisten from tears you cry.

It's hard to see a Mummy leave,
feels like hearts in two do cleave.
The pain is there each every day,
we try our best to hide away.

In quiet moments for 13 years,
reliving moments that gave us cheers.
Things we deemed a special day.
Fathers giving brides away.

Grandchildren born to your great joy,
little girl or little boy.
Christmas Birthdays Easter fun,
made great by you each every one.

In quiet moments for 13 years,
words to heaven about our fears.
Our prayers we know that she can hear,
sends us Angels to banish fear.

She was my Grandma and your Mum,
our hearts flow over with memories done.
Prizes won for costumes made,
flowered floats in town parade.

Seen by many if not all,
Gwen's girls in the carnival.
She filled our lives with lots of fun,
look at all the memories done.

Skittle teams that ruled the alley,
four daughters Gran and our Callie.
Those many nights you laughed out tears,
remembered fondly these 13 years.

We think of you with hearts and mind,
the thoughts are always loving kind.
In quiet moments when day is done,
she was my Grandma and your Mum.

76. Jesus, Jesus.

Jesus, Jesus, where are you,
look at what your people do.
Lost their way in the dark,
words of love we fail to hark.

Kill and plunder rape and spoil,
poison skies water soil.
Caught in hunger for our greed,
desire for objects we don't need.

Wandered off or righteous path,
hear that devil with his laugh.
Jesus, Jesus can't you see,
what God's image has come to be.

Killers crooks and greedy men,
world in ruin once again.
Angels once filled all the skies.
now in darkness despair cries.

Lost their way and forgot the lore,
gold and silver hoards to store.
No longer try to do what's right,
no care for walking in the light.

Jesus, Jesus, why did you go,
left us all to turn out so.
Without your righteous guiding light,
temptation leads to dark deeds night.

Lust and envy jealous rage,
released all demons from hells cage.
Devils whisper in our ear,
your Angels words we no longer hear.

World gone mad in pointless war,
all because the rich want more.
Jesus, Jesus please come back,
reset mankind back on the track.

Rescue man before too late,
come lock the chains on hells gate.
The deeds we do so cruel and many,
it seems compassion we haven't any.

The good and kind persecuted,
God's own words too long been muted.
Such hate from man to fellow man,
the flames that burn so pleased to fan.

Jesus, Jesus, the world gone wild,
lost to world the innocent child.
War zones famine disease and drought,
is this Gods judgement we see about.

I think it is Devils plan,
to corrupt Lords image of made man.
Come intervene before too late,
slowdown the queue at Heaven gate.

Descend those stairs from heavens hall,
Come back to earth and save us all.
We need you now to stand with us,
Be born again Jesus, Jesus.

77. What words.

What words shall I use,
what can I say.
So sorry to hear,
of your loss today.

You've lost someone special,
that stood by your side.
You thought that forever,
they'd share the whole ride.

I'm sending you love,
and sympathy too.
Who knows the reasons,
for things Angels do.

What words shall I use,
what can I say.
You've lost your best friend,
been stolen away.

Taken to heaven,
for reasons not known.
Up amongst Angels,
for God now to own.

I feel all your sadness,
and see broken hearts.
The pain is so blinding,
when a loved one departs.

What words shall I use,
what can I say.
Will it make any difference,
or ease pain away.

Left alone standing,
with lost wonder why.
Who makes decisions,
on who has to die.

The Angels all gather,
to witness the deed.
Yet another from earth,
who's soul has been freed.

What words shall I use,
what can I say.
Who can offer the comfort,
to you on this day.

Your soul mate was taken,
your partner in crime.
Lifted up to the heavens,
I guess it was time.

Time for the Angels,
to light a new star.
That shines down on us,
from high up afar.

What words shall I use,
what can I say.
Who's arms will you now,
at night your head lay.

Left alone in the darkness,
hearts heavy with sigh.
Just a pillow for hugging,
catching tears that you cry.

Life can be unfair,
when left alone.
Last picture you took,
last text to your phone.

What words shall I use,
what can I say.
I'll ask Angels for you,
tonight when I pray.

I'll ask for some guidance,
for some reason why.
I'll plead for their comfort,
to tears that you cry.

I'll get them to show you,
a new star in sky.
When you see it shining,
you'll know reasons why.

What words shall I use,
what can I say.
They make the hard choices,
on who cannot stay.

The light of your life,
was needed above.
See how it shines,
and shares out the love.

That love that you filled it,
so full every day.
What words shall I use,
what can I say.

78. Grim Reaper soul seeker.

Grim Reaper soul seeker,
is that you that I see.
Hid in the shadows,
stood watching me.

I'm tired of the struggle,
and weak from the fight.
Drained from dark thoughts,
in my head every night.

Grim Reaper soul seeker,
life so unfair.
I've tried much too hard,
for no one to care.

Down the dark pit,
a place I know well.
Each person carries,
their own private hell.

Grim Reaper soul seeker,
where do you go.
Your dark shroud of death,
you so like to throw.

Come cast it my way,
and smother this life.
Come melt all the worries,
and soothe all the strife.

Grim Reaper soul seeker,
please come and claim.
This life full of hardships,
and struggle through pain.

So tired of all failures,
of doing things wrong.
Come reap me you bastard,
I just can't go on.

Grim Reaper soul seeker,
please answer my call.
I'm willing and ready,
into your arms to fall.

All that I do,
I seem to do wrong.
I can't see the point,
in continuing on.

Grim Reaper soul seeker,
come claim my soul.
I'm tired of the blame,
for each every own goal.

I've tried to endeavour,
my aim was to please.
But each every failure,
knocks down to my knees.

Grim Reaper soul seeker,
that's it I'm done.
Life's lost its sparkle,
it's no longer fun.

Dark pit of depression,
once more claims me.
How hard I have struggled,
failed to break free.

Grim Reaper soul seeker,
I've lost all the will.
All I've attempted,
a battle up hill.

I'm ready for sleep,
the peace of the grave.
To catch your attention,
your notice I crave.

Grim Reaper soul seeker,
come take my hand.
My soul's lost its sparkle,
you do understand.

You stand right before me,
dark stare meets my eye.
You're refusal to take me,
it's not time to die.

Grim Reaper soul seeker,
why are you so mean.
You've witnessed my life,
and all it has been.

Is it no wonder I'm tired,
my spirits so low.
Are you really so shocked,
that I'm ready to go.

Grim Reaper soul seeker,
don't turn your back.
Please take my soul,
to stash in your sack.

Left alone standing,
you're fading from view.
So many others,
you've taken with you.

Grim Reaper soul seeker,
it looks like I've failed.
The ferry man paid,
with pennies has sailed.

You've walked away smiling,
I've made your day.
The first time a soul,
not wanting to stay.

Grim Reaper soul seeker,
I provide you the mirth.
Will you really condemn me,
to life on this Earth.

My time yet to come,
so far, far away.
You shun my appeal,
and leave me to stay.

Grim Reaper soul seeker,
the words that you said.
Fifty more years,
until I am dead.

Fifty more years,
of life left to live.
Who decided how many,
years to me give.

Grim Reaper soul seeker,
you've left me to fall.
To wait half a century,
until next time you call.

The ferry man ferries,
across oceans of tears.
Oceans I'll fill,
for fifty more years.

Grim Reaper soul seeker,
my all that I gave.
My life you won't take,
a soul you don't save.

The reasons for living,
they grow ever weaker.
I'm ripe for the harvest,
Grim Reaper soul seeker.

79. What lies beyond.

What lies beyond,
our final sleep.
Who clams our souls,
as theirs to keep.

How far and high,
do spirits fly.
What follows after,
our time to die.

Does the soul linger,
on sad memories.
Once life has faded,
is the spirit at ease.

Does it watch over,
those that will mourn.
Is it thrown back,
a new life reborn.

Did you make heaven,
that wonderful place.
Perhaps start out new,
of past life no trace.

Are you walking with Angels,
earning your wings.
Escaped from this earth,
and the woe that it brings.

What lies beyond,
our final sleep.
Who claims our souls,
as theirs to keep.

Does your memory still carry,
all of our names.
Do you chuckle out loud,
when you remember our games.

When a soul leaves a body,
does it carry past deeds.
Reach heaven empty,
a vessel without needs.

I'd like to know truly,
if all that we do.
Is left at the gates,
or carried through.

In quiet dark evenings,
when I lay alone.
Thoughts of mortality,
and lost friends are prone.

How far and how high,
do spirits fly.
What follows after,
our time to die.

Are you gone forever,
do you no longer exist.
Is darkness oblivion,
the final cruel twist.

What matters the struggle,
of right or wrong.
If nothing comes after,
a soul moves along.

Surely there's something,
some reward for the fight.
It can't just be darkness,
no sounds in the night.

There must be some Angels,
or some kind reward.
All good deeds done,
must have points scored.

What lies beyond,
our final sleep.
Who claims our souls,
as theirs to keep.

The good go to heaven,
the repenting ones too.
This is the end game,
to all that we do.

The bad we want punished,
those that have fell.
Denied heavens entry,
sent down to hell.

All of it's hearsay,
no proof it is true.
The belief or the doubt,
resides within you.

Does it truly matter,
want to believe.
Maybe there's really nothing,
once a soul chose to leave.

How far and how high,
do spirits fly.
What follows after,
our time to die.

Long peaceful darkness,
no feelings or thought.
Without recollection,
of answers once sought.

Just suspended in darkness,
like dust inside ice.
Peaceful eternity,
my that sounds nice.

No struggle or battle,
decisions to be made.
No worried anxiety,
or reasons afraid.

But who knows you're nothing,
just a speck in the dark.
God it's confusing,
this after life lark.

What lies beyond,
our final sleep.
Who claims our souls,
as theirs to keep.

There has to be something,
this I'll believe.
For if there was nothing,
why would a soul leave.

The secrets are hidden,
revealed when we die.
Who are we really,
to ask questions why.

The decision of heaven,
reincarnation or hell.
It's not for mere mortals,
to know of or tell.

It's choices of Angels,
that watch over you.
They take continuous notes,
on all that you do.

How far and how high,
do spirits fly.
What follows after,
our time to die.

When comes the moment,
It's your turn to die.
You'll stand before God,
and know reasons why.

You'll be given all answers,
to all questions asked.
And judged by the deeds,
through the life you were tasked.

You could be admitted to heaven,
or sent down to hell.
Perhaps earn some wings,
if you hear rung bell.

If the decision is balanced,
to the Gods contemplation.
Then sent back to earth,
via reincarnation.

Sean Michael McCarthy

What lies beyond,
our final sleep.
Who claims our souls,
as theirs to keep.

What are the answers,
who knows what's right.
Am I believing in heaven,
well maybe I might.

It gives me some comfort,
for when comes my ends.
I may step through the gates,
be met by old friends.

I believe we are Angels,
out earning our wings.
Via trials of this life,
and all that it brings.

My friends I shall ask them,
why couldn't they see.
Just a whisper from heaven,
from them down to me.

Would have solved all the riddles,
made jigsaw complete.
Eased all the worries,
if there's Angels to meet.

What lies beyond,
our final sleep.
Who claims our souls,
as theirs to keep.

How far and high,
do spirits fly.
What follows after,
our time to die.

The answer is heaven,
pure paradise.
To be held by almighty,
if we're deemed nice.

Up past the moon,
behind stars in the sky.
To shine on forever,
eternally fly.

80. Spirit crushed.

Spirit crushed and soul destroyed,
consequence of love enjoyed.
D and Y then I N G,
everything inside of me.

My mind the devil screams inside,
prompting thoughts of suicide.
Surely I'd be better dead,
away from thoughts inside my head.

Guardian Angel abandoned post,
just as I did need the most.
Why were you not stood beside,
I needed you to safely guide.

Lost and trembling like new born child,
fend for self in world gone wild.
Spirit crushed and soul destroyed,
empty shell of played and toyed.

Took a chance exposed my heart,
ripped to shreds and torn apart.
Spirit crushed and soul destroyed,
where once was love now barren void.

Turmoil beats inside my chest,
my faith again is given test.
God above me looking down,
tired of this sad circus clown.

Have my efforts you amused,
again my trust has been abused.
I should have stayed behind my wall,
rejected approach of lovers call.

I was so foolish to believe,
I should have known that you would leave.
No sooner had the words been said,
came the moment all hearts dread.

Dreams of wonder and happy heart,
would have better not let start.
What made me think that I could fly,
rebuild my walls go way up high.

High enough to merge with cloud,
let no one in it's not allowed.
Each time I do I seem to fail,
all that time to no avail.

Spirits crushed and soul destroyed,
why did these feelings I not avoid.
Hide in shadows don't be seen,
cast aside this longing dream.

Keep adding bricks to the wall,
hide away from one and all.
Build it faster build it high,
keep out players and all who lie.

Staying single safe to be,
no more heart inside of me.
Took it out and buried deep,
never will you make me weep.

Not once more shall I believe,
nor wear my heart upon my sleeve.
Sacked my Angel she's not employed,
spirit crushed and soul destroyed.

81. Do you ever.

Do you ever feel unwanted,
like an empty bottle of wine.
Do you ever feel discarded,
spend with you no time.

Do you ever feel avoided,
there's always some excuse.
Do you ever feel abandoned,
let go set free cut loose.

Do you ever feel all lonely,
sat on sofa all alone.
Do you ever see the hermit,
sitting silent in your home.

Do you ever think life's over,
when left all by yourself.
Do you ever share out love,
by far the greatest wealth.

Do you ever even wonder,
what I do when left alone.
Do you ever check your pocket,
for my message on your phone

Do you ever understand why,
without you I don't sleep.
Do you ever comprehend,
that I want to safe you keep.

Sean Michael McCarthy

Do you ever get a feeling,
it's time that you came back.
Do you ever even realise,
your time has lost the track.

Do you ever even miss me,
when your out and I'm not there.
Do you ever want to kiss me,
run my fingers through your hair.

Do you ever want to cuddle,
with me upon our bed.
Do you ever share your deep thoughts,
that drift inside your head.

Do you ever listen clearly,
to the words that I now say.
Do you ever feel rejected,
when all alone you lay.

Do you ever want me with you,
walking hand in hand.
Do you ever give your shadow,
next to me to stand.

Do you ever think to wonder,
or stop to reason why.
Do you ever see the hurt,
or hear my hearts sad sigh.

Do you ever even cotton on,
that I sit up and I wait.
Do you ever catch an inkling,
that I worry when you're late.

Do you ever stop to ponder,
what I do when left at home.
Do you ever take a minute,
to send a quick text to my phone.

Do you ever feel unwanted,
like an empty bottle of wine.
Do you ever feel discarded,
like I do at this time.

82. The world through rainbow tears.

Stuck in Peter Pan mode, never growing old

I'm stuck in Peter Pan mode,
never growing old.
My brain is wired different,
or so I'm always told.

I have no fear of danger,
I fail to see the threat.
There's no demons in my shadows,
out for me to get.

I've lost the key to Never Land,
will I ever get it back.
I'm stuck outside of paradise,
lost the way home track.

My mind is full of innocence,
no anguish fear or woe.
The world is full of rainbows,
everywhere I go.

You jump at all the shadows,
the ones I fail to see.
Your outlooks always cautious,
It's better being me.

I smile and laugh at pictures,
I see inside my head.
You think that I am special,
needing guidance must be led.

Can't you see I'm normal,
like Angels in the sky.
Living life with laughter,
with spirits flying high.

Who's to say I'm different,
and not original.
How are you so certain,
It's not you that's dropped the ball.

You fell on down from heaven,
it left you full of dread.
It must have been a long drop,
did you land upon your head.

My mind it sees a rainbow,
in the smile of every child.
You label me as simple,
autistic folder I get filed.

I'm not a word or label,
but pure love of heavens hall.
Let go from the Never Land,
to help all those that fall.

My mind is always busy,
counting up the deeds.
Reports I send to Angels,
who tally up the needs.

The numbers whirl round faster,
more and more each day.
Is it any wonder,
I fill my days in play.

I keep my thoughts so simple,
the innocence of young.
It helps to process info,
and hear what's needing done.

Stripped right down to the basics,
what everybody needs.
Sleep and love and laughter,
ensure the spirit feeds.

I'm stuck in Peter Pan mode,
It doesn't mean I'm dumb.
My mind is swamped by colours,
it sends my conscience numb.

I see and I remember,
the world through rainbow tears.
You don't see magic colours,
lost in shadows of your fears.

You chase around in circles,
lost keys to Never Land.
All alone in darkness,
your lonely spirit stand.

Endless is your wonder,
of Angels in the sky.
Tumbling goes your turmoil,
and your questions why.

Cherubs fill the paradise,
floating through the skies.
Singing songs of love,
with pure soul lullabies.

I see the world in colour,
bright and clear and pure.
Brush away the shadows,
at fingertips the cure.

You fail to see the beauty,
a sky so clear and blue.
I cry my tears of rainbows,
lost magic you once knew.

Why did I leave my Never Land,
my world of Peter Pan.
Trapped forever childlike,
inside body of a man.

This world is not for Angels,
It's cruel towards my kind.
I hide behind the colours,
that swirl inside my mind.

I hear the music playing,
the song of every word.
I miss the soft sweet lullabies,
I once in heaven heard.

These eyes that see through rainbows,
rich colours drip the tears.
Keep my mind protected,
from reality and It's fears.

Yet still you fail to see,
you just can't understand.
I walk without my shadow,
left safe in Never Land.

Held by threads of magic,
spun in purest gold.
Connects my soul to spirit,
forever years back hold.

Not aging like the others,
neither body nor my mind.
Youthful spirit is eternal,
until that key I find.

The child you think so different,
all reasons you are told.
Is stuck in Peter Pan mode,
never growing old.

83. Did you know.

Did you know that you would leave us,
did you know that you would die.
Did you have to keep it secret,
did you want to tell us why.

You've stepped into the shadows,
of our memories yesterday.
Took that ride upon the ferry,
a small copper paid the way.

You left us all just standing,
lost in search of reasons why.
Who up there in heaven,
gets to choose the ones to die.

Did you know that you would leave us,
did you know that you would die.
Did you have to keep it secret,
did you want to tell us why

They seem to scoop up all the loved ones,
no matter who's left sad.
Woe the little children,
who have lost to God their Dad.

Never mind the family,
or the lifelong friend.
These things are not considered,
when Angels call the end.

Did you know that you would leave us,
did you know that you would die.
Did you have to keep it secret,
did you want to tell us why.

The void you left is massive,
a hole we'll never fill.
We didn't even realise,
how serious was your ill.

I think of you in moments,
when quiet and alone.
It's hard to grasp reality,
you're never coming home.

Did you know that you would leave us,
did you know that you would die.
Did you have to keep it secret,
did you want to tell us why.

You struggled on through suffering,
and never said a word.
My heart it just stopped beating,
when the sad news told was heard.

Your shadow has stopped struggling,
and soul gave up the fight.
The Angels deemed you worthy,
to go with them that night.

Did you know that you would leave us,
did you know that you would die.
Did you have to keep it secret,
did you want to tell us why.

We stood around in silence,
counting out our tears.
Surreal is astonishment,
uncertain in our fears.

How will life continue,
without you standing by.
Can a heart keep beating,
when drowned by tears we cry.

Did you know that you would leave us,
did you know that you would die.
Did you have to keep it secret,
did you want to tell us why.

Small comfort are the memories,
magic moments shared in time.
Do they give you quiet chuckles,
as you queue in heavens line.

Our bonds and threads of magic,
thin and stretch and snap.
As the through the gates of heaven,
you go with no look back.

Did you know that you would leave us,
did you know that you would die.
Did you have to keep it secret,
did you want to tell us why.

We're left with all the pieces,
scattered shattered on the floor.
Eyes are now all empty,
no tears to cry no more.

We sweep up all the moments,
we shared throughout the years.
And stick together memories,
bonded strong with our wept tears.

Did you know that you would leave us,
did you know that you would die.
Did you have to keep it secret,
did you want to tell us why.

And when in quiet moments,
you drift like ghost through mind.
It's with such loving memory,
our souls can some peace find.

We know you're with the Angels,
no longer feeling pain.
Accept that life without you,
can never be the same.

Did you have to keep it secret,
did you want to tell us why.
Was it written in the contract,
by Angels in the sky.

Did you know that you would leave us,
did you know that you would die.
Can you hear these I send you,
farewell my friend, goodbye.

84. Whispers.

Can you hear the whispers,
the whispers in the trees.
The flights of Guardian Angels,
are stirring up a breeze.

They battle with the Demons,
that hide within the shade.
A conflict very ancient,
once more being played.

Can you hear the whispers,
the voices in your head.
They offer you temptation,
with lies that you are fed.

Promises of glory,
riches and of fame.
The tricks they use to trip you,
usually end with pain.

Can you hear the whispers,
the whispers in the trees.
The flights of Guardian Angels,
are stirring up a breeze.

Shadows from our Angels,
are not for us to see.
The battle and the conflict,
to set our spirits free.

The hell of indecision,
lure of too much choice.
Ignore the Demons whispers,
hark pure the Angels voice.

The words you know as wisdom,
come from soul within.
Stand faith as high as heaven,
don't let the lure begin.

Can you hear the whispers,
the whispers in the trees.
The flights of Guardian Angels,
are stirring up a breeze.

We each of us have Angels,
that try so hard to please.
Can you hear their whispers,
they whisper through the trees.

Repent the wrong decisions,
bad choices that you made.
Got led by Demons voices,
abused you as they played.

The path they showed looked easy,
a quick route to success.
They leave you standing empty,
ruined, wrecked, a mess.

Can you hear the whispers,
the whispers in the trees.
The flights of Guardian Angels,
are stirring up a breeze.

Call down your Guardian Angel,
pray guidance of the light.
Hear whispers through the tree tops,
that's them come down to fight.

They'll battle with your Demons,
they bring the word of God.
The melt away of turmoil,
as binding chains are shod.

Good will always conquer,
when fed with faith and trust.
The light upon your shoulder,
just listen to you must.

Can you hear the whispers,
the whispers through the trees.
The words so pure and loving,
from Angels in the breeze.

Each shun of dark temptation,
adds strength to their new wings.
The ever climb on upwards,
hear how the heaven sings.

Slow spirals ever higher,
adrift beyond the trees.
Left whispers in the branches,
that guard your spirits free.

They fall upon your shoulder,
and whisper in your ear.
They banish all your worries,
protect the soul from fear.

Can you hear the whispers,
the whispers in the trees.
The flights of Guardian Angels,
are stirring up a breeze.

85. The pit.

When you look into a mirror,
tell me what you see.
When you glance in my direction,
do you see the same in me.

We all of us have demons,
that whisper in our ear.
They try to drown out Angels,
words for us to hear.

When we're fine and feeling happy,
and life it goes all right.
Avoiding pull of darkness,
such struggle in the night.

The silent slip to blackness,
depressions deep dark well.
Such weight upon our shoulders,
when we carry our own hell.

With smiles and fake fun laughter,
we paper over cracks.
The demons in the shadows,
so sudden their attacks.

We walk along with millions,
never felt this so alone.
realization jumps upon us,
heavy heart is made of stone.

So crowded is the bottom,
futility the spell.
Dark and damp surroundings,
no echo to our yell.

When you look into a mirror,
tell me what you see.
When you glance in my direction,
do you see the same in me.

We all of us have demons,
that whisper in our ear.
They try to drown out Angels,
words for us to hear.

When we're fine and feeling happy,
and life it goes all right.
Avoiding pull of darkness,
such struggle in the night.

Why does it come and grab us,
sink in claws so very deep.
My outside appearing happy,
whilst inside a soul does weep.

The storm so soon upon us,
skies once blue turn grey.
I wonder how long these feelings,
will this time choose to stay.

So many are the reasons,
but pin point we can't find.
Vast distance comes the journey,
so hard the back up grind.

Always when we're happy,
come the monsters in the night.
Whispers from dark shadows,
blocking out the light.

Demons hate to see us,
free and having fun.
They trip and send us tumbling,
and laugh at what they've done.

Knocked back on down the ladder,
that took so long to climb.
Back amongst the lost souls,
groping sightless in the grime.

Despair to find a hand hold,
to grip that bottom rung.
The determined once more effort,
once more escape begun.

When you look into a mirror,
tell me what you see.
When you glance in my direction,
do you see the same in me.

We all of us have demons,
that whisper in our ear.
They try to drown out Angels,
words for us to hear.

When we're fine and feeling happy,
and life it goes all right.
Avoiding pull of darkness,
such struggle in the night.

The devil never gives up,
he doesn't like to lose.
He'll suck you down the dark pit,
the timing his to choose.

The battle of your life time,
once more the endless loop.
Away from darkened outlook,
your lost souls final scoop.

One hand upon the ladder,
then two and next your feet.
So slow the climb is upwards,
survival waits to greet.

So frequent is this journey,
lost count the times I fell.
Please God guide my direction,
come shepherd me from hell.

For me there's nothing greater,
than the morning after night.
Fought my way through darkness,
to once more reach the light.

Did anybody notice,
did they see that I had fell.
Have Angels stood to witness,
my triumphant flee from hell.

So weary from the battle,
the way back hard and long.
But my spirit is unbeaten,
my soul once more stands strong.

Every time it grabs me,
every slide back down the pit.
Makes me more determined,
and stronger after it.

I won't let hells dark shadows,
drag or keep me down.
You'll not my light extinguish,
or my purpose drown.

We walk amongst the millions,
and trick you with our smiles.
But hidden on the inside,
each person battles trials.

Don't take it all as granted,
each smile you see is true.
Stop and ask the question,
with hey and how are you.

Sometimes just a soft word,
can halt that final tread.
Deviate direction,
and shatter all the dread.

Always are the moments,
and wonder who does care.
That's darkness in the shadows,
malice with his despair.

When you look into a mirror,
tell me what you see.
When you glance in my direction,
do you see the same in me.

We all of us have demons,
that whisper in our ear.
They try to drown out Angels,
words for us to hear.

When we're fine and feeling happy,
and life it goes all right.
Avoiding pull of darkness,
such struggle in the night.

86. Today they say.

It's Father's day

Today they say is Father's day,
the time to think of dad.
To show some love with words you say,
but for me it's kind of sad.

I've lived through half a century,
50 long hard years.
Was this life really meant for me,
distance drowned in tears.

My children grown and moved away,
the trip 9 thousand miles.
It often feels like yesterday,
they were babies full of smiles.

My memory full of shadows past,
moments caught in time.
Over quick the ever last,
our magic was so fine.

Today they say is Father's day,
the time to think of dad.
To show some love with words you say,
but for me it's kind of sad.

Faster do the years go by,
one to five then ten.
How quickly does the time soon fly,
turns life to way back when.

We cling to thoughts of happy days,
let sadness drift and fade.
Fun we had in crazy ways,
so short the time we played.

Life without so incomplete,
with children up and gone.
Shadows on an empty street,
the lonely walk along.

Today they say is Father's day,
the time to think of dad.
To show some love with words you say,
but for me it's kind of sad.

My children gone not standing near,
they've grown and moved away.
Eyes that sparkle full of tear,
cards I'm dealt to play.

Nine thousand miles separates,
3 kiddies from their dad.
Busy life with new mates,
remembered love we had.

I tried to fill their lives with fun,
but wish I had done more.
I'm feeling not enough was done,
and judge my efforts poor.

Today they say is Father's day,
the time to think of dad.
To show some love with words you say,
but for me it's kind of sad.

Time once thought as moving slow,
was speeding blink of eye.
Where did those magic moments go,
when laughter made us cry.

I carry love inside my heart,
your spirits fill my soul.
The world between keeps us apart,
your creation made me whole.

I hope your children think of you,
more than once a year.
Nine thousand miles the message through,
come glisten out that tear.

Today they say is Father's day,
the time to think of dad.
To show some love with words you say,
but for me it's kind of sad

87. Magic wonder.

There's fairies in the night woods,
and Angels in the trees.
The magic once abundant,
lost floating on the breeze.

Such wonder and amazement,
glory for the eyes.
The things that lifted spirits,
dissolved into the skies.

What secrets to believe in,
the superstitious fact.
Who walks beneath a ladder,
avoids a pavements crack.

The pixies in the garden,
the dwarfs that mine the moon.
A Genie in a bottle,
with wish to grant a boon.

A star up high to wish on,
the cloverleaf of four.
A lucky silver horse shoe,
to hang upon a door.

Who salutes the single magpie,
crosses fingers for good luck.
Who leans into the wishing well,
to lucky penny chuck.

Sean Michael McCarthy

We find a lucky pebble,
with a shape we've never seen.
Add to the collection pot,
the one that's full of dream.

The troll beneath an old bridge,
pooh sticks to pay the toll.
Such little magic rituals,
engraved upon our soul.

Magic from our childhood,
reluctant to believe.
Discarded by the roadside,
as on through life we weave.

Do giants march by moonlight,
the woods of walking trees.
Fairies riding bareback,
on their bumbles we call bees.

Who believes that the rainbows,
will lead to pots of gold.
Folklore, myths and legends,
our imagination holds.

Back when we were little,
three years since we were born.
Each of us would dreams take,
of rides on unicorn.

We'd visit lands of chocolate,
with streets of ginger bread.
Endless was the magic,
that floated in our head.

The trust we had in Angels,
that floated in the sky.
Eternal ever guarding,
from birth until we die.

Let's not forget the dragons,
the kings of all the land.
Who has the recollection,
of sights of wonder grand.

What world of magic wonder,
do they go to when they die.
These things that stop existing,
when belief has all run dry.

There's fairies in the night woods,
and Angels in the trees.
The magic once abundant,
lost floating on the breeze.

Such wonder and amazement,
glory for the eyes.
The things that lifted spirits,
dissolved into the skies.

88. Where are you now.

Where are you now,
what do you do.
Is life fulfilled,
did dreams come true.

Are friends still friends,
if never seen.
That magic lost,
like never been.

So many times,
we'd laugh and cry.
All lost in time,
as years slip by.

Sometimes we see,
a reminding face.
Or pass on through,
a once went place.

A stop to think,
in memory find.
A name long lost,
slow ghost through mind.

The wonder what,
and where for why.
Are you alive,
or did you die.

Where are you now,
what do you do.
Is life fulfilled,
did dreams come true.

Are friends still friends,
if never seen.
That magic lost,
like never been.

Do spirits know,
or hearts still break.
If one once loved,
did Angels take.

The magic fades,
it drifts away.
Like morning mists,
of yesterday.

Hearts we held,
so whole complete.
Turned to dust,
around our feet.

Sean Michael McCarthy

Friends let go,
or lovers lost.
The lonely soul,
that carries cost.

Where are you now,
what do you do.
Is life fulfilled,
did dreams come true.

Are friends still friends,
if never seen.
That magic lost,
like never been.

The drift apart,
the passing day.
Weeks then months,
in years we pay.

Who knows the names,
of friends slipped by.
Lost forever,
what reasons why.

Where did you go,
what do you do.
Who shares your laughs,
and loves you true.

Who holds your hand,
when life has woe.
Now stands beside,
shares sun shines glow.

Where are you now,
what do you do.
Is life fulfilled,
did dreams come true.

Are friends still friends,
if never seen.
That magic lost,
like never been.

89. Abandoned Angels.

My wings have turned to shadow,
they crumble into dust.
My guiding light once needed,
now discarded left to rust.

Who takes the time to realize,
I'm gone no longer here.
Does my absence cause emotion,
or bring to eye a tear.

I'm just a buried memory,
not real I don't exist.
No longer in your conscious thoughts,
a name removed from list.

Do you ponder on the question,
why me you haven't seen.
Am I archived recollection,
a ghost to drift through dream.

I'm a face you see in shadows,
a merge into the crowd.
A name not quite remembered,
no recognise allowed.

Once no longer needed,
so quick I'm left to fall.
Omitted from your night prayer,
lost promise you would call.

I'm insignificant notice,
no remarkable to note.
My words go said un-spoken,
crumpled unread note.

Surplus to requirements,
a fashion not the trend.
How quickly are discarded,
those we once called friend.

Lost from circulation,
crowded out of life.
Suddenly the effort,
hard work and too much strife.

Am I fade inside of memory,
a feeble grasp at straws.
Is deja-vu the recognise,
when my eyes grab hold of yours.

Was I someone of importance,
a reliance you once knew.
is recollection leaking in,
knowledge seeped slow through.

This yesterday of shadow,
that once would answer call.
So often came the rescue,
from each and every fall.

I note your stop to ponder,
I see your search through time.
The battle through lost memory,
you know a name that's mine.

Too long has been the moment,
the slow drift part of ways.
Lost beyond the counting,
piled high the wasted days.

Merged into the background,
no substance worth the note.
Melted into history,
blank pages nothing wrote.

My wings have turned to shadow,
they crumble into dust.
My guiding light once needed,
now discarded left to rust.

Who takes the time to realize,
I'm gone no longer here.
Does my absence cause emotion,
or bring to eye a tear.

I'm just a buried memory,
not real I don't exist.
No longer in your conscious thoughts,
a name removed from list.

Do you ponder on the question,
why me you haven't seen.
Am I archived recollection,
a ghost to drift through dream.

90. Such sorrow is the moment.

Am I doom across the mountains,
the storm above the sea.
Am I thunder am I lightening,
why do you hide from me.

Am I snow drifts over feelings,
do I blizzard all thoughts out.
Do my tears flood your patience,
what's this silence all about.

Such sorrow is the moment,
when romance comes to end.
Bitter builds resentment,
with loss of once dear friend.

Who pulls the final curtain,
decides it's time to run.
How long has indecision,
blocked out all the sun.

Now lonely like the last leaf,
that clings to winters tree.
Abandoned like a sailor,
shipwrecked lost at sea.

I sit lost at my window,
watch the world go by.
The silence like a prison,
holding tears I cry.

Solitary single,
now just me all by myself.
Lost in pointless dreaming,
like dust upon a shelf.

The magic gone it faded,
the laughs had all run dry.
Continuous the effort,
flames flicker and then die.

Such sorrow is the moment,
when romance comes to end.
Bitter builds resentment,
with loss of once dear friend.

Who pulls the final curtain,
decides it's time to run.
How long has indecision,
blocked out all the sun.

So silent are the strong ones,
stoic in their stance.
Seeking out dark corners,
no spirit left to dance.

Who notices one tear drop,
upon the desert sand.
Who hears the quietest note,
when playing in the band.

Sitting at the window,
the glass begins to steam.
Lost the silent wonder,
on all we could have been.

Now stands a single shadow,
under moon of silver light.
Who hears the silent sorrows,
the cries hid by the night.

Such sorrow is the moment,
when romance comes to end.
Bitter builds resentment,
with loss of once dear friend.

Who pulls the final curtain,
decides it's time to run.
How long has indecision,
blocked out all the sun.

Hear how my footsteps echo,
the walk through life alone.
No more loving messages,
showing on my phone.

Sometimes things are over,
the magic was all used.
The reasons insignificant,
left standing all confused.

Such sorrow for the hurt caused,
the sorrow for the pain.
But once the magic dwindles,
things just never seem the same.

The hope that anger spares us,
when finally comes the end.
Waiting for the smoke to clear,
and leave behind a friend.

Am I doom across the mountains,
the storm above the sea.
Am I thunder am I lightening,
why do you hide from me.

Am I snow drifts over feelings,
do I blizzard all thoughts out.
Do my tears flood your patience,
what's this silence all about.

Such sorrow is the moment,
when romance comes to end.
Bitter builds resentment,
with loss of once dear friend.

Who pulls the final curtain,
decides it's time to run.
How long has indecision,
blocked out all the sun.

91. Stolen our Angel

You've stolen our Angel,
taken our one.
Snatched from our hearts,
what have you done.

Left us all hurting,
with questions why.
Is it true that you needed,
a new star for your sky.

We look to the heavens,
with hearts heavy sigh.
Our Angel too young,
that you've chosen to die.

The life that you ended,
had barely begun.
So full of love,
laughter and fun.

Is it fair that you leave us,
with holes to the heart.
Dreams turned to ashes,
and life torn apart.

You've stolen our Angel,
turned off the light.
Snatched from our hearts,
it's surely not right.

This life once had laughter,
love and no fears.
Now full of sadness,
eyes flooded with tears.

Why do you claim them,
the innocent young.
Snatched from their living,
what have you done.

All hearts are now hurting,
they mourn and they yearn.
What is this lesson,
you send us to learn.

The ones we deem precious,
that fill life with love.
Are they truly the ones,
heaven needs up above.

You've stolen our Angel,
she stands by your side.
She runs for your comfort,
with arms open wide.

Our hearts are so heavy,
the beats are so slow.
It was too soon,
for our Angel to go.

We walk on in circles,
lost deep in thought.
Questions we're asking,
answers are sought.

Why take our Angel,
we can't understand.
Was it an accident,
or something you planned.

Does truly your night sky,
need a new star.
Is that why you've taken,
our brightest by far.

You've stolen our Angel,
it leaves us all sad.
So precious the moments,
and short time we had.

With minds full of memory,
and hearts full of pride.
We know that our Angel,
is stood by your side.

So watch us from heaven,
and feel all our love.
Shine on forever,
in skies up above.

The hurt will stay with us,
our tears slowly dry.
The reason above us,
with Angels that fly.

Goodbye precious daughter,
so long our dear friend.
Take with you our wishes,
and love that we send.

With wings white and pure,
and halo of gold.
You've stolen our Angel,
she's yours now to hold.

92. Mothers cry.

Questions asked for reasons why,
every year when comes July.
Attention lost in deep sad thought,
why you the Angels chased and caught.

Your ghost he comes to drift through mind,
the search so hard to meaning find.
Sitting staring lost in space,
inside our mind your smiling face.

You haven't changed you're just the same,
how long can hearts keep holding pain.
Such loss we feel come month July,
the 15th day that you did die.

Your life was full of laughs and fun,
so many things we shared and done.
Why did you leave why did you go,
how could the Angels hurt us so.

Cousin Rumbo, brother, son,
we hope your heaven is full of fun.
It's 14 years since Angels came,
took you to heavens halls of fame.

Left all behind with tears to cry,
un-answered questions for reasons why.
In blink of eye the time has past,
this pain from loss does ever last.

Your drift to mind is often many,
Aunty Karin, Denise and Penny.
Cousins left and cousins right,
all think of you this day and night.

Father ponders and Mothers cry,
endless tears when children die.
Brother Moddy saw you go,
endless are his nights of woe.

It's still all hard to understand,
why did Angels take your hand.
Could they not see all our love,
choose some other to take above.

Lonely moments moonlit sky,
such are times of questions why.
Riding solo down a road,
feel the loss inside explode.

Thoughts that drift and find your face,
hesitation halts the pace.
Stop to think and wonder why,
look to heaven in the sky.

Oh cousin Rumbo feel our pain,
life has not quite been the same.
Something missing some part lost,
a piece of heart we paid in cost.

Questions asked for reasons why,
every year this day in July.
Attention lost in deep sad thought,
why you the Angels chased and caught.

Your ghost he comes to drift through mind,
the search so hard to meaning find.
Sitting staring lost in space,
inside our mind your smiling face.

93. Oh what a day.

The wedding came,
oh what a day.
Magic moment,
I do they say.

Eyes that meet,
in love they stare.
Lost in wonder,
are all stood there.

The happy smiles,
and tears of joy.
Cherish this moment,
of girl and boy.

They tie the knot,
and make the bond.
Two hearts now one,
forever fond.

Oh sing out loud,
and share the glee.
The love now set,
for eternity.

Oh what a day,
and perfect match.
Each is thrilled,
by their catch.

Sean Michael McCarthy

Whispered vows,
exchange of rings.
Church so full,
hear how it sings.

Walk the aisle,
hear the cheers.
Mum and Dad,
wiping tears.

The sun now shines,
on two joined one.
Adventure starts,
new life begun.

Hand in hand,
side by side.
Hearts so full,
the love and pride.

Oh what a day,
new start to life.
Happy husband,
and his wife.

94. A Heart.

A heart remembers,
all feelings felt.
Always there,
the bruises dealt.

The pain received,
wrongs once done.
Live in shadows,
clinging on.

A heart recalls,
each happy day.
Sad recalls,
the take away.

The broken moment,
stuck in time.
Like stab with knife,
as Devils dine.

A heart will ponder,
on what went wrong.
Such hurting pain,
it lasts so long.

Shattered dreams,
future lost.
Count the tears,
weigh the cost.

　　　Sean Michael McCarthy

A heart that's broken,
so slow to mend.
Loss of lover,
goodbye the friend.

The pain of sorrow,
an empty soul.
Walk on blindly,
search for goal.

A heart once cherished,
then dropped to floor.
The want to cease,
no beat no more.

Life continues,
most things heal.
But hearts remember,
the pain stays real.

A heart that beats,
slow plod along.
A sudden heavy,
broke, gone wrong.

The shadow pounces,
it gives no warn.
The wish to heaven,
to not be born.

The heart, my heart,
the curse of life.
Carries moments,
re-lives strife.

Silent shadows,
cover bruise.
Pain reminder,
of all you lose.

Words of promise,
quick burn to embers.
All feelings felt,
a heart remembers.

95. My Flower.

Goodbye my flower,
farewell my heart.
You called the end,
again must start.

I gave my soul,
for 5 whole years.
You throw away,
whilst crying tears.

Cast aside,
scant overlook.
Turned to ash,
my heart you took.

I lost your soul,
through fingers slip.
No light soft kiss,
of gentle lip.

Now see two souls,
that once were one.
Cruel split in half,
it's over. Done.

With easy breeze,
you walk away.
No glance back,
the end you say.

How did it turn,
oh so wrong.
All that love,
where has it gone.

From high to low,
so fast the fall.
The choice was made,
not mine to call.

A slow walk off,
to fading sun.
A life once shared,
now faded, done.

The leave behind,
of family.
A lonely path,
my shadow me.

You carry on,
brave face and smile.
My fade from mind,
so short the while.

I last a minute,
or maybe hour.
Goodbye my heart,
farewell my flower.

Sean Michael McCarthy

96. These thoughts, these thoughts.

These thoughts, these thoughts,
inside my head.
Dreams we shared,
and words once said.

These thoughts, these thoughts,
the endless loop.
Shattered dreams,
how low your stoop.

These thoughts, these thoughts,
of all gone wrong.
The radio plays,
our once loved song.

These thoughts, these thoughts,
oh please just stop.
Once was precious,
so quick to drop.

These thoughts, these thoughts,
they grind me down.
How quick can kings,
slip lose their crown.

These thoughts, these thoughts,
such turmoil many.
Reasons sought,
no finding any.

These thoughts, these thoughts,
they torture soul.
Where once flood over,
now empty bowl.

These thoughts, these thoughts,
inside my mind.
New reason life,
must quick soon find.

These thoughts, these thoughts,
they torture me.
The hammer thumps,
the quest for free.

These thoughts, these thoughts,
that scream so loud.
Darkness decent,
so cool the shroud.

These thoughts, these thoughts,
such endless pain.
How can life,
now be the same.

Sean Michael McCarthy

These thoughts, these thoughts,
must let them go.
Breath so deep,
heart beat slow.

These thoughts, these thoughts,
those words I read.
Echo endless,
inside my head.

These thoughts, these thoughts,
in endless toy.
Remembered pleasures,
that bring no joy.

These thoughts, these thoughts,
with you I share.
Heart laid open,
a soul to bare.

These thoughts, these thoughts,
my words can't tell.
Inside my mind,
it burns like hell.

These thoughts, these thoughts,
I pray for end.
Soft gentle hands,
come my soul tend.

These thoughts, these thoughts,
see what they do.
The screams out loud,
attention you.

Dreams we shared,
and words once said.
These thoughts, these thoughts,
inside my head.

97. Dreamed dark thoughts.

These dreamed dark thoughts,
inside my head.
To close ones eyes,
brings on such dread.

The world once mine,
is lost to me.
Gone all chance,
and destiny.

Snatched from grip,
and thrown to floor.
Cases packed,
and shown the door.

Lost the way,
no will to fight.
Left alone,
in silent night.

Sat on the curb,
my cooling rain.
Washes spirit,
down into drain.

Who can see,
this soul laid bare.
None come forth,
no love nor care.

In happy jig,
at job well done.
Battle lost,
to mothers son.

So sly the plan,
from long past start.
The creeping shadow,
of poisoned heart.

Such battle long,
repeat the try.
Requests refused,
so bitter why.

In corner dark,
now curled alone.
Hearts have turned,
such heavy stone.

Warmth did drain,
and fade away.
Words once meant,
no longer stay.

The I love you,
just passes by.
Disregard,
and no reply.

I gave my best,
and all my power.
Yet still I failed,
to save my flower.

She faded fast,
withheld her scent.
So 5 long years,
now wasted spent.

It's over now,
the words were said.
These dreamed dark thoughts,
inside my head.

98. Pedestal.

Steps once used,
to pedestal.
How high it seems,
now to fall.

How once I felt,
that I could fly.
Immortal soul,
to never die.

Now cut the strings,
that held me right.
Abandoned arms,
once fastened tight.

Left alone,
in life to fend.
Who is left,
to my heart tend.

Cast aside,
and thrown away.
Will this pain,
a long time stay.

Sean Michael McCarthy

Steps once used,
to pedestal.
Heart strings broke,
so cruel the pull.

Head hangs down,
oh where to start.
So cruel the hurt,
that stabs my heart.

Path once clear,
a surface bright.
This way blocked,
closed this night.

My brain all mist,
thick fog to eye.
Stop the breathes,
just let me die.

No strength to stand,
now time to fall.
Descend the steps,
once pedestal.

99. Will Angels Wings.

Will Angels wings,
still fly when broke.
Can tears drown,
the soul to choke.

Will laughter come,
oh faded dream.
Happy thoughts,
the once had been.

Will sadness close,
such tired eyes.
Heart beats rhythm,
between the sighs.

Will pain we feel,
in endless ebb.
Such tremors felt,
cruel life web.

Will such dark thoughts,
inside my head.
Grant peaceful leave,
as love lies dead.

Will tears they count,
in thousand years.
The light shine down,
and banish fears.

Sean Michael McCarthy

Will Angels sigh,
when sorrow felt.
So cruel the cards,
and harshly dealt.

Will skies turn blue,
slow fades the grey.
How can at night,
in sleep I lay.

Will answers find,
my searching thought.
How quick let fall,
my heart once caught.

Will pain soon fade,
all kind words spoke.
Will Angels wings,
still fly when broke.

100. Spiral down.

See the face,
fall spiral down.
Head hung low,
so hides the frown.

See the tears,
that stain the cheek.
Words to mouth,
the fail to speak.

See the heart,
now still it's beat.
Lost desire,
no fate to meet.

See the shudder,
and shoulder shake.
Hear soft cries,
the sorrow make.

See despair,
how stripped the soul.
When lost the chance,
fulfil life goal.

See the lost,
the wandered way.
What power love,
in hearts do slay.

Sean Michael McCarthy

See the hope,
melt like mist.
Hands clutch air,
with empty fist.

See the dreams,
now turned so stale.
Feel the pain,
A heart impale.

See the woe,
of all in me.
Please take the hurt,
and set me free.

See the loss,
and wonder why.
Count the tears,
so clouds the eye.

See the sad,
in circus clown.
See me drop,
fall spiral down.

101. My World Once Full.

My world once full,
is now no more.
Shattered pieces,
across the floor.

My heart once whole,
now withered dry.
Tears have flooded,
all run by.

Dreams once shared,
all turned to dust.
Future bright,
now pitted rust.

Demons lost,
and cast away.
Returned once more,
to my heart slay.

Passions once,
that burned like fire.
Faded embers,
of lost desire.

No longer wanted,
lost the need.
Darkness creeps,
come to feed.

Lost the way,
my path now dark.
Hear hells hounds,
howl and bark.

Sean Michael McCarthy

My world once full,
now empty bleak.
Lost loves words,
no longer speak.

Embers fade,
to slowly die.
The door slammed shut,
no hear the cry.

I sit alone,
in corner dark.
My world turned bleak,
the lonely stark.

I'm cast away,
like daydream thought.
Slip through hands,
the heart once caught.

Abandoned soul,
a spirit broke.
Tears that drown,
and slowly choke.

Shattered pieces,
across the floor.
My world once full,
is now no more.

102. Captured moments.

Those captured moments,
caught in time.
Happy faces,
when all was fine.

Photo albums,
pictured wall.
All unaware,
soon comes the fall.

We were younger,
so in love.
Angels smiling,
watch above.

Holidays,
and honeymoon.
Perfect moments,
gone too soon.

Happy child,
caught in glee.
Foster love,
with you and me.

Sean Michael McCarthy

The once was us,
gone and lost.
Broken heart,
that pays the cost.

Am I to blame,
was all my fault.
You hit me with,
a lightening bolt.

It struck me down,
as I stood strong.
I didn't know,
life was wrong.

Thrown away,
without a fight.
Told by letter,
in dead of night.
I worked too hard,
the bills to pay.
I didn't see,
your slip away.

I held your hair,
when you were sick.
I thought our bond,
was strong and thick.

I carried through,
when you were ill.
My love embers,
they flicker still.

My gold dust lover,
don't understand.
How what we had,
could slip through hand.

I never meant,
to make you cry.
You never told me,
I don't know why.

Did you see,
it slip away.
Each every precious,
happy day.

You say you knew,
this passing year.
I was deaf,
I couldn't hear.

To busy working,
paying bill.
My care for you,
whilst you was ill.

I didn't know,
I couldn't see.
I'm left alone,
abandoned me.

Forgive my fail,
it wasn't meant.
Those captured moments,
in love we spent.

103. Stepped into the shadows.

I've stepped into the shadows,
I'm avoiding all the light.
My movements are restricted,
hid by darkness of the night.

I want to go unnoticed,
unseen by single eye.
Hid in gloomy blackness,
so none can see me cry.

Wounds so fresh and hurting,
they open up old scars.
Lost all magic moments,
smashed all memory jars.

I walk in dizzy ponder,
and wonder what went wrong.
The silent slow slip under,
the loss of all belong.

Please understand my silence,
if you've ever had a fall.
You'll see there is no wonder,
at adding bricks to wall.

That's it, no more forever,
the promised love you gave.
Words no longer have a meaning,
broken vows you will not save.

We use to fly like Angels,
with hearts so full of trust.
You abandoned all our magic,
left all in crumbled dust.

The battle of the death throws,
hurt then pain and woe.
Bitterness and anger,
how easy you let go.

You leave without a battle,
no warning did you give.
Just left alone in darkness,
with all this pain to live.

Love turns to quick resentment,
affections freezing cold.
Remove your heart from my hands,
no longer precious hold.

Take your spirit from my conscience,
strip my soul to best friend bare.
Let the magic fade to history,
no longer do you care.

The deed you've done is wicked,
a decision far from right.
I've stepped into the shadows,
I'm avoiding all the light.

104. No longer.

No longer the cleaner,
no longer the cook.
No longer to see,
my money all took.

No longer a chauffeur,
nor shopping man.
No longer the home help,
doing all that I can.

No longer the step dad,
nor Foster dad too.
No longer that long list,
of house chores to do.

No longer the washing,
to get done all wrong.
No longer the ironing,
that took me so long.

No longer the struggle,
to get all bills paid.
No longer the ill wife,
with love for me fade.

No longer will I,
so struggle for sleep.
With worries for you,
all to safe keep.

No balancing books,
or max credit card.
The struggle was long,
survival so hard.

No matter what done,
I always seemed wrong.
No complaints did I give,
I just struggled on.

No love from your son,
no ounce of respect.
But always in comfort,
your hallways were decked.

No moments of passion,
no loving me still.
Husband replaced,
to care for your ill.

No longer the school runs,
each morning and day.
Now after night shifts,
in sleep I can lay.

No giving up every,
hobby and friend.
So you in your illness,
I can care for and tend.

No more will my interests,
and all I did dream.
Be left on the back burn,
like never had been.

No more will my children,
not see their Dad.
I can travel down under,
no longer be sad.

No longer your husband,
no longer with wife.
No longer just working,
I now can live life.

No longer the sadness,
that's it for me.
No longer am trapped,
once more I am free.

105. Passing shadow.

I'm just a passing shadow,
a flicker to the eye.
I ghost across your vision,
not noticed passing by.

My existence is in limbo,
I'm a shadow hid by shade.
My soul that once shone brightly,
how fast does magic fade.

The future that once was certain,
step by step we had a plan.
How quick we lost the blue print,
destiny flushed down the pan.

I'm living life in moments,
frozen memories in my head.
Turmoil of confusion,
so cold the water tread.

I've lost all understanding,
can't fathom reasons why.
The cries we send to heaven,
to question Angels why.

I'm just a passing shadow,
where no one knows my name.
My echoed lonely footsteps,
the beat to mask the pain.

To walk around in silence,
all the faces stand unknown.
Surrounded by so many,
yet still to feel alone.

The world that once embraced me,
now stripped away and lost.
The love once shared abandoned,
cast out to bare the cost.

I never stopped my loving,
and yet i had to leave.
Was i just a captive,
deceitful web you weave.

No thought of me is taken.
no empathy to show.
You've banished me to history,
a shadow you let go.

106. I walk along.

I walk along,
in lost despair.
Heading home,
to no one there.

Silent steps,
my head hung down.
To ghost alone,
the drift through town.

The happy sounds,
seep into night.
Crush my heart,
a squeeze so tight.

A chink of light,
through curtains gap.
Goodnight cuddle,
from child on lap.

I walk along,
and pass on by.
Such things now lost,
what reasons why.

The chimneys smoke,
from family fire.
All vows once sworn,
abandoned liar.

I worked and worked,
missed out on life.
Provided home,
for children wife.

No time to live,
no thought for me.
All friends forgot,
this busy bee.

I walk along,
the lonely street.
To empty room,
where none shall greet.

The home we shared,
and slowly built.
You have it all,
and show no guilt.

No longer loved,
sad but true.
We're over now,
finished through.

No warning sign,
no attempt to save.
A son unhappy,
the reason gave.

I walk along,
all by myself.
Our happy pictures,
removed from shelf.

Now cut from life,
all contact stopped.
See how fast,
a heart is dropped.

So soon ignored,
and left alone.
All trace is washed,
away from home.

Our foster child,
I'd come to love.
Not seen no more,
away the shove.

I walk along,
the streets at night.
I've lost the will,
there's no more fight.

One man alone,
in strangers town.
Head hung low,
and eyes kept down.

People swerve,
step out the way.
Lost are words,
what can they say.

I worked so hard,
I gave my all.
You were my Angel,
on pedestal.

I walk along,
up to my room.
To lay on bed,
such thoughts of doom.

The quiet dark,
such silence heard.
No hello honey,
or welcome word.

What weight the hurt,
who measures scales.
So heavy a heart,
when full of fails.

You see I knew,
that things were wrong.
Now left alone,
I walk along.

107. Shelley Dee.

The joy she brings to Angels,
the gift that you let go.
Love spread throughout the heavens,
shared for all to know.

Your tiny bundle of happiness,
so scant the moment here.
Heaven chooses special ones,
leaving loving eyes to tear.

The love you gave in moments,
would fill a thousand hearts.
The loss and hopeless feeling,
wonder over at its starts.

We carry love forever,
inside deep where none can see.
The memory lasts like magic,
dear precious Shelley Dee.

108. Listen, see and understand.

Where have thirty years gone,
how hindsight tortures me.
All the things I've done wrong,
lost all possibility.

The silence from the shadows,
cast by long set sun.
Thoughts drifting back to yesterday,
and things we should have done.

So scant the magic moments,
smothered faded by hard life.
The echo of our laughter,
drowned by noise and strife.

A heart that bursts from first kiss,
electric shock from holding hand.
Why would we let that future go,
listen, see and understand.

Where have thirty years gone,
how hindsight tortures me.
All the things I've done wrong,
lost all possibility.

We all of us have crossroads,
many turns that we took wrong.
Remembered indecision,
memory jogged by favoured song.

Who here would turn a clock back,
choose paths a different way.
Maybe hold that hand tight,
kept forever here to stay.

Life happens for a reason,
all good as well as bad.
This life we have is too short,
for putting up with sad.

A heart that bursts from first kiss,
electric shock from holding hand.
Why would we let that future go,
listen, see and understand.

Where have thirty years gone,
how hindsight tortures me.
All the things I've done wrong,
lost all possibility.

We each inside have demons,
and all of us chase dreams.
Step out from cloudy drizzles,
run naked through sun beams.

Identify those moments,
the ones that lift your soul.
Making your heart happy,
is number one the goal.

Get up and chase that rainbow,
search out your pot of gold.
When you capture magic moments,
be sure to grab tight hold.

A heart that bursts from first kiss,
electric shock from holding hand.
Why would we let that future go,
listen, see and understand.

Where have thirty years gone,
how hindsight tortures me.
All the things I've done wrong,
lost all possibility.

If life is always struggle,
constant seems the woe.
Then destiny's still waiting,
it's time to change let go.

Search through hindsight moments,
seek the love laughter.
That flicker warmth can still flame,
the happy ever after.

A once upon a time tale,
can be yours to now create.
Life passes by too quickly,
so hurry grab your fate.

A heart that bursts from first kiss,
electric shock from holding hand.
Why would we let that future go,
listen, see and understand.

109. I close my eyes in daydream.

I close my eyes in day dream,
the memory of your face.
The warmth spread from your laughter,
your hand in mine you place.

Your company it lifts me,
lost soul you guide to path.
Each moment seems like magic,
when you share your laugh.

To see the winter sunset,
fall across your face.
Stars glitter in your kind eyes,
my heart is set to race.

The smile that you give me,
when I call to you your name.
Such comfort understanding,
we've shared such lives the same.

I close my eyes in day dream,
the memory of your face.
The warmth spread from your laughter,
your hand in mine you place.

We've both had hardship journeys,
a year gone past of woe.
See now we circle wagons,
how high our walls now go.

Sean Michael McCarthy

The doubt and indecisions,
the loss of self-esteem.
The fragments lay so scattered,
how can again we dream.

To see the winter sunset,
fall across your face.
Stars glitter in your kind eyes,
my heart is set to race.

Each moment seems perfection,
when time is spent with you.
Is it need coincidental,
or feelings real and true.

I close my eyes in day dream,
the memory of your face.
The warmth spread from your laughter,
your hand in mine you place.

The hurts all heal in instant,
and demons they all fade.
The sharing of our memories,
the times we laughed and played.

You leave me feeling happy,
yet sad when time to go.
Counting minutes by the heartbeat,
spirits lifted they now glow.

The smile that you give me,
when I call to you your name.
Such comfort understanding,
we've shared such lives the same.

A life of short perfection,
the years go flashing by.
We each of us need laughter,
to be the tears we cry.

I close my eyes in day dream,
the memory of your face.
The warmth spread from your laughter,
your hand in mine you place.

I stand behind horizon,
and hide my awe of you.
I think my heart has eyes on,
the one dream it wants so true.

My patience will be virtue,
I'm certain of the choice.
The Angel on my shoulder,
whispered sweetness inner voice.

Your company it lifts me,
lost soul you guide to path.
Each moment seems like magic,
when you share your laugh.

You'll see these words I've written,
and know they're meant for you.
Too long we've run from shadows,
of things we know as true.

Karma, fate or fortune,
these things that should have been.
Your face and warmth of laughter,
I close my eyes and dream.

110. Every time a shadow.

Every time a shadow,
shields the sunshine from your eye.
It's me I'm now an Angel,
Slowly gliding by.

With you every moment,
watching all you do.
Our hearts still full of love,
forever they'll stay true.

Every time a rainbow,
falls across your sky.
It's love that i am sending,
to help to stop you cry.

With you whilst you're sleeping,
to sentry guard your dream.
Sending happy memories,
of all the joy that's been.

Every time a soft breeze,
comes cool caress your brow.
It's my gentle breath from kisses,
with you here and now.

With you like a shadow,
each and every day.
I hear the words you whisper,
each night time as you pray.

Every time that pillow,
receives your tearful squeeze.
I whisper soothing lullabies,
sleep my lover please.

With you and within in,
throughout your soul and mind.
Close your eyes and dream my dear,
and you will soon me find.

Every time you stumble,
caught by moments feeling sad.
Look back on us in fondness,
and smile at all we had.

With you all life was magic,
so full of love and fun.
The wings i have in heaven,
they come from all we've done.

Every time a shadow,
shields the sunshine from your eye.
It's me I'm now an Angel,
Slowly gliding by.

111. The sweetest of words.

Tiny the bundles, that jump up for hugs

The sweetest of words,
I ever did hear.
Were when getting home,
and "daddy is here".

The running small feet,
that patter the floor.
In such magic moments,
a heart wants no more.

Tiny the bundles,
that jump up for hugs.
They show you their pictures,
of dragons and bugs.

You offer them kisses,
and ruffle their hair.
Such is their joy,
from having you there.

These moments perfection,
in life all is good.
Re live them forever,
if only you could.

Time it soon passes,
in blink of an eye.
Such welcome home rituals,
slow fade then pass by.

Those little lost Angels,
now ghosts back in time.
Where once we were happy,
and all life was fine.

The years they come age us,
and distance does part.
We dream back with longing,
and loss in the heart.

The sweetest of words,
I ever did hear.
Were when getting home,
and "daddy is here".

The running small feet,
that patter the floor.
In such magic moments,
a heart wants no more.

112. Unsuitable that end.

How soothing flow the waters,
from the springs of hope.
Step down away from danger,
and leave that swinging rope.

Resist that dark temptation,
unsuitable that end.
Duty bound continuation,
who else your hearts will tend.

Insignificant solution,
such selfishness of deed.
Who will console the children,
that you will always need.

There's light at end of tunnel,
it's just around the bend.
Let me ease the burden,
come lean on me my friend.

I'll carry you through rivers,
that flow so deep with pain.
Lift you over mountains,
that you climb again.

Feel the warmth of sunshine,
grip tight the helping hand.
I recognize the struggle,
and true do understand.

Some battles they seem endless,
and stuck in endless loop.
Leave you buried inside misery,
so slow the up-hill troop.

Sean Michael McCarthy

How soothing flow the waters,
from the springs of hope.
Step down away from danger,
and leave that swinging rope.

Resist that dark temptation,
unsuitable that end.
Duty bound continuation,
who else your hearts will tend.

You offer life some purpose,
some difference you do make.
Stand strong against the darkness,
resist that lure so fake.

We all of us have options,
the choice of deeds we do.
The Angels they have notions,
and future plans for you.

They test you with the battles,
resolve of yours they try.
Skirt the edge of dark pits,
refuse the call to die.

Keep strong and pure your focus,
stay pure within the heart.
This world with you not finished,
the future yours to start.

The Devil lays his dark lures,
he tries to catch your eye.
Succumb to his temptation,
you'll leave a world in cry.

How soothing flow the waters,
from the springs of hope.
Step down away from danger,
and leave that swinging rope.

Resist that dark temptation,
unsuitable that end.
Duty bound continuation,
who else your hearts will tend.

I see your shoulders shaking,
the burden of your load.
So blistered are your footsteps,
the hardship of the road.

The world looks on in wonder,
amazed you still fight on.
So many would drown under,
and leave the world be gone.

The shadows are so many,
and walls we climb so high.
Stay strong my friend and fight on,
resist that call to die.

We each of us are Angels,
on earth to battle sin.
Stay pure and walk in sunshine,
the conflict we can win.

Inside your quiet moments,
when you think you stand alone.
Call out your words of help me,
I'll come help you atone.

How soothing flow the waters,
from the springs of hope.
Step down away from danger,
and leave that swinging rope.

Resist that dark temptation,
unsuitable that end.
Duty bound continuation,
who else your hearts will tend.

Insignificant solution,
such selfishness of deed.
Who will console the children,
that you will always need.

There's light at end of tunnel,
it's just around the bend.
Let me ease the burden,
come lean on me my friend.

I'll carry you through rivers,
that flow so deep with pain.
Lift you over mountains,
that you climb again.

Feel the warmth of sunshine,
grip tight the helping hand.
I recognize the struggle,
and true do understand.

Some battles they seem endless,
and stuck in endless loop.
Leave you buried under misery,
so slow the up-hill troop.

How soothing flow the waters,
from the springs of hope.
Step down away from danger,
and leave that swinging rope.

Resist that dark temptation,
unsuitable that end.
Duty bound continuation,
who else your hearts will tend.

You offer life some purpose,
some difference you do make.
Stand strong against the darkness,
resist that lure so fake.

We all of us have options,
the choice of deeds we do.
The Angels they have notions,
and future plans for you.

They test you with the battles,
resolve of yours they try.
Skirt the edge of dark pits,
refuse the call to die.

Keep strong and pure your focus,
stay pure within the heart.
This world with you not finished,
the future yours to start.

The Devil lays his dark lures,
he tries to catch your eye.
Succumb to his temptation,
you'll leave a world in cry.

How soothing flow the waters,
from the springs of hope.
Step down away from danger,
and leave that swinging rope.

Resist that dark temptation,
unsuitable that end.
Duty bound continuation,
who else your hearts will tend.

113. The biting winds of winter.

So golden hue the colour,
and crisp the winter leaf.
Our superficial pretence,
well hides what's underneath.

The biting winds of winter,
pretend a summers breeze.
How simple we deceive you,
trick you with such ease.

Our outside always laughing,
so easy fake the smile.
Whilst spirits battle Demons,
the inner turmoil trial.

The world upon the outside,
brief glance with no look in.
Our masks of gold grow heavy,
resistance stretched so thin.

The strides we take are heavy,
with legs that weigh like lead.
So full of life our image,
whilst inside all is dead.

Our hearts once full of passion,
now cold and turned to stone.
Surrounded by some millions,
yet feel we stand alone.

Sean Michael McCarthy

So golden hue the colour,
and crisp the winter leaf.
Our superficial pretence,
well hides what's underneath.

The biting winds of winter,
pretend a summers breeze.
How simple we deceive you,
trick you with such ease.

Not one can hear the echo's,
my screams lost in the wind.
The rain disguises tear drops,
eyes once bright now dimmed.

The bleakness of a winter,
fast freeze of passions burn.
Is it gentle slip to darkness,
that the tortured soul does yearn.

Like branches of a great oak,
once full now nothing there.
Stripped of summer sunshine,
lost passion and will to care.

So constant is the onslaught,
that lay my branches bare.
Once life so full and fruitful,
resigned with no more care.

So golden hue the colour,
and crisp the winter leaf.
Our superficial pretence,
well hides what's underneath.

The biting winds of winter,
pretend a summers breeze.
How simple we deceive you,
trick you with such ease.

The world so rich in colour,
like forests of Autumn leaves.
Overlooked by passing karma,
we wipe our tears with sleeves.

Foundations rooted certain,
once deep now full of rot.
Cruel twist the fate and fortune,
the loss of all once got.

What think you distant thunder,
hear you my anguish cries.
Clouds darken the horizons,
with hearts of heavy sighs.

Our outside always laughing,
so easy fake the smile.
Whilst spirits battle Demons,
the inner turmoil trial.

So golden hue the colour,
and crisp the winter leaf.
Our superficial pretence,
well hides what's underneath.

The biting winds of winter,
pretend a summers breeze.
How simple we deceive you,
trick you with such ease.

The world upon the outside,
brief glance with no look in.
Our masks of gold grow heavy,
resistance stretched so thin.

The strides we take are heavy,
with legs that weigh like lead.
So full of life our image,
whilst inside all is dead.

Our hearts once full of passion,
now cold and turned to stone.
Surrounded by some millions,
yet feel we stand alone.

Not one can hear the echo's,
my screams lost in the wind.
The rain disguises tear drops,
eyes once bright now dimmed.

So golden hue the colour,
and crisp the winter leaf.
Our superficial pretence,
well hides what's underneath.

The biting winds of winter,
pretend a summers breeze.
How simple we deceive you,
trick you with such ease.

The bleakness of a winter,
fast freeze of passions burn.
Is it gentle slip to darkness,
that the tortured soul does yearn.

Like branches of a great oak,
once full now nothing there.
Stripped of summer sunshine,
lost passion and will to care.

See how I sit in silence,
eyes lost in distant gaze.
Why has the world abandoned,
and stolen my whole amaze.

A life of half a century,
with little left to show.
The slow slip of the seasons,
the loss of summers glow.

Sean Michael McCarthy

So golden hue the colour,
and crisp the winter leaf.
Our superficial pretence,
well hides what's underneath.

The biting winds of winter,
pretend a summers breeze.
How simple we deceive you,
trick you with such ease.

So bitter builds resentment,
like winds on tundra steep.
Ignored like homeless orphans,
alone at night we weep.

A winter sun can shine bright,
but warmth it offers none.
The battle never ending,
tortured memories of things done.

Come please my Guardian Angel,
with welcome arms so wide.
I need your strength to carry,
the hurt and loss inside.

Come free this soul from winter,
your love can melt the ice.
Snap the gloom away from dark thoughts,
show me something to entice.

So golden hue the colour,
and crisp the winter leaf.
Our superficial pretence,
well hides what's underneath.

The biting winds of winter,
pretend a summers breeze.
How simple we deceive you,
trick you with such ease.

New purpose or direction,
new bud or planted seed.
Something new of your creation,
my soul it has the need.

See how I sit in silence,
eyes lost in distant gaze.
Why has the world abandoned,
and stolen my whole amaze.

A life of half a century,
with little left to show.
The slow slip of the seasons,
the loss of summers glow.

So bitter builds resentment,
like winds on tundra steep.
Ignored like homeless orphans,
alone at night we weep.

So golden hue the colour,
and crisp the winter leaf.
Our superficial pretence,
well hides what's underneath.

The biting winds of winter,
pretend a summers breeze.
How simple we deceive you,
trick you with such ease.

A winter sun can shine bright,
but warmth it offers none.
The battle never ending,
tortured memories of things done.

Come please my Guardian Angel,
with welcome arms so wide.
I need your strength to carry,
the hurt and loss inside.

Come free this soul from winter,
your love can melt the ice.
Snap the gloom of dark thoughts,
show me something to entice.

New purpose or direction,
new bud or planted seed.
Something new of your creation,
my soul it has the need.

So golden hue the colour,
and crisp the winter leaf.
Our superficial pretence,
well hides what's underneath.

The biting winds of winter,
pretend a summers breeze.
How simple we deceive you,
trick you with such ease.

Sean Michael McCarthy

114. So brief the walk in sunshine.

So brief the walk in sunshine,
how quick the light can fade.
Left alone within the solitude,
with memories that we made.

With laughter's echo fading,
weakened image in the mind.
Are choices made the correct ones,
or just cruelty being kind.

When you find yourself unwanted,
will it heaviness the heart.
Or change your steps directions,
begin a brand new start.

Each every shut the door makes,
it moves to free a space.
Opens up new highways,
which down your feet can pace.

So brief the walk in sunshine,
how quick the light can fade.
Left alone within the solitude,
with memories that we made.

Searching endless for perfection,
fulfilment of the soul.
Like grains of sand through fingers,
see how the dice can roll.

Passing by goes some temptation,
is it harbour for your storm.
Left behind with contemplation,
what reasons where you born.

See sparkled diamond star dust,
in the laughter of your eyes.
The welcome of distraction,
some comfort for the cries.

So brief the walk in sunshine,
how quick the light can fade.
Left alone within the solitude,
with memories that we made.

The burdens that we carry,
us each and every one.
Seem light and unsubstantial,
when hearts are having fun.

To those that truly notice,
and take the time to care.
Thank you for your kind words,
it's good to know you're there.

My spirit full of promise,
optimistic my middle name.
No longer am I governed,
I refuse to feel more pain.

Sean Michael McCarthy

So brief the walk in sunshine,
how quick the light can fade.
Left alone within the solitude,
with memories that we made.

New dreams I am inventing,
adventures to begin.
The soul's determination,
bursts out from deep within.

You showed me true potential,
by giving freely your belief.
Pulled away all shadows,
revealed the real me hid beneath.

No need not now no longer,
loss the stumble in my stride.
Returned my self-sufficient,
lifted heart you filled with pride.

So brief the walk in sunshine,
how quick the light can fade.
Left alone within the solitude,
with memories that we made.

115. Has life become a shipwreck.

Has life become a shipwreck,
on the bottom of the sea,
Are you floating soul survivor,
scared and all lonely.

Are the bubbles all around you,
the screams of things you've done.
Or the joyful shouts of triumph,
from the Devil thinks he's won.

Feel the drag of history,
it tries to pull you down.
Let go the ghosts in memory,
they overwhelm and drown.

Do you float just treading water,
in the hope that help will come.
Are there others floating with you,
do you feel the only one.

Are those stars on the horizon,
or a distant rescue ship.
Will help come with salvation,
before under waves you slip.

Has life become a shipwreck,
on the bottom of the sea,
Are you floating soul survivor,
scared and all lonely.

You cling to floating drift wood,
with arms that slowly numb.
Life in flash-back reveals all,
is all over what just begun.

The dreams you had are sinking,
trapped like souls in hell.
The lights below are fading,
final chime upon ships bell.

The choices now have dwindled,
stay sink or begin the swim.
With prayers to God above you,
you lay your life with him.

May he send you down an Angel,
to help to guide your way.
Please Lord think of my children,
don't drown my soul today.

The stars up in the night sky,
they slowly start to fade.
Your arms and legs so heavy,
how quick the spirits jade.

Has life become a shipwreck,
on the bottom of the sea,
Are you floating soul survivor,
scared and all lonely.

Who's witness to your efforts,
only birds that shrill above.
What's left upon this world today,
who now for you to love.

A light breaks the horizon,
the sunshine greets your soul.
Oh how you miss the solid land,
upon which once you'd stroll.

What thought you distant thunder,
it's hypnotising beat.
Are they waves upon the shore line,
that they smash and greet.

Numb fingers brush the wet sand,
like gold dust to your feel.
Am I dead or am I dreaming,
please God let this be real.

Legs so weak from all the effort,
knees that will not bend.
With final blast of will power,
drag free from waters end.

Has life become a shipwreck,
on the bottom of the sea,
Are you floating soul survivor,
scared and all lonely.

The cool wet sand of safety,
now pressed against your cheek.
Now salt the tears of wonder,
thank you to Lord you speak.

Survivor of a ship wrecked,
out lived the life you lost.
Let go beneath the oceans,
but alive to count the cost.

Time to walk some new lands,
fresh beaches to explore.
Eyes gaze at fresh horizons,
new strangers at the door.

Forget the memories lost now,
leave them bottom of the sea.
Open eyes to new chance,
and all possibility.

Has life become a shipwreck,
on the bottom of the sea,
Are you floating soul survivor,
come walk the world with me.

116. Stare at corners.

I sit and stare at corners,
my mind is lost in space.
Where once a heart was beating,
now lays a cold dark place.

My mind once full of day dreams,
and plans of things to do.
Stripped of magic inspiring,
used up and empty through.

I'm going through the motions,
fake smiles to hide the woe.
Stay hid amongst the shadows,
until these Demons go.

Empathy, compassion,
Angels plans of destiny.
Has karma changed opinion,
gone, abandoned me.

The smile you gave was rescue,
like reach to drowning man.
I grasped too hard and squeezed tight,
it's no wonder that you ran.

Not fear or desperation,
just needing deeply for a friend.
I sit and stare at corners,
when will this lonely end.

Who knows what comes tomorrow,
we have to wait and see.
Can you tell and see just how much,
your hello means to me.

To go from all to nothing,
is a mighty way to fall.
Endless is the tumble,
stopped by text or call.

I sit and stare at corners,
my mind is frozen bare.
Empty as a night sky,
would seem with no stars there.

It's not the heart that's hurting,
for that in time does heal.
It's the feeling of abandoned,
when all alone I feel.

Do your thoughts give me a mention,
or my name tug on your heart.
Would you like to ask me questions,
but don't know how to start.

I'm the same friend that you once knew,
before the spanner thrown.
Don't leave me sitting staring,
at corners on my own.

Just knowing that you see me,
that I truly still exist.
Can ease the pain called lonely,
remove that knifes cruel twist.

I need that special contact,
a smile of friendly face.
Steer me away from corners,
and stop my stare in space.

117. Frantic grasp.

The frantic grasp for fibres,
so few the threads of hope.
Un wind the strands so binding,
cut free constricting rope.

Release the bonds that shackle,
set free the captured soul.
Pull clear the knots that burden,
unravel, free, unroll.

The weight of chains that cripple,
like anchors through the heart.
A sucking grip like quicksand,
the stop of every start.

The frantic grasp for fibres,
so few the threads of hope.
Un wind the strands so binding,
cut free constricting rope.

The struggle for the surface,
how long can your breath hold.
Long absence of warm comfort,
alone and lost and cold.

Shrug off the bonds that smother,
escape the holding back.
The light at end of tunnel,
just around that bend in track.

The frantic grasp for fibres,
so few the threads of hope.
Un wind the strands so binding,
cut free constricting rope.

Held back by deeds uncertain,
buried alive by all gone wrong.
Passed by go happy faces,
their hearts so full of song.

The edge of doom it crumbles,
tries hard to slip you in.
Step back from your oblivion,
don't let the darkness win.

The frantic grasp for fibres,
so few the threads of hope.
Un wind the strands so binding,
cut free constricting rope.

With ties to past discarded,
deep breaths of final free.
The chains that held abandoned,
to face that all will be.

The journey won't be easy,
many the trips and fall.
But all the choices offered,
now mine I'm free for all.

The frantic grasp for fibres,
so few the threads of hope.
Un wind the strands so binding,
cut free constricting rope.

118. When you see me in your dream.

I hope I make you happy,
when you see me in your dream.
I'll melt away your rain clouds,
and send you sunshine beam.

I'll fill your eyes with star dust,
flood happy in your mind.
Bring love to all your corners,
light up all I find.

I hope I make you happy,
when you see me in your dream.
Had destiny took chances,
the things that could have been.

Tell me does your heart skip,
when you hear my name.
Do thoughts of me in passing,
set insides aflame.

I hope I make you happy,
when you see me in your dream.
I see the way you watch me,
like a cat that wants the cream.

How quickly does your pulse race,
when I throw to you my smile.
Does my memory stay and linger,
when parted for a while.

I hope I make you happy,
when you see me in your dream.
Does life just sometimes hit you,
it's not what should have been.

Can you remember how it tingled,
when we shared that sweet first kiss.
That feeling that my insides,
forever more has missed.

See memory how it tortures,
with things long past and been.
I hope I make you happy,
when you see me in your dream.

119. The sadness of the Day.

The sadness of the day,
it comes to reach us all.
The Angels came for Father,
he had his curtain call.

The loss and feeling lonely,
the frozen heart so scared.
We knew this time would catch us,
but still caught un-prepared.

Goodbye to dear old Daddy,
farewell to our first chum.
We shared the tears of laughter,
and many times of fun.

The Angels up in heaven,
they've set another place.
The time to take it easy,
the end of your long race.

The loss we feel is hurting,
a numbness to the soul.
A game of life has ended,
robbed of winning goal.

He stood with me forever,
a lifetime by my side.
Opened the horizons,
Showed a world so wide.

Taught to me my courage,
showed me how to care.
My empathy, compassion,
it's him that put it there.

Another rock we cling to,
has slipped beneath the sea.
We hope that heavens hallways,
offer sunshine, shade for thee.

The sadness of the day,
it comes to reach us all.
The Angels came for Father,
he had his curtain call.

120. Storms were never ending.

You may have stood and watched,
the roughness of my sea.
The storms were never ending,
kept trying to drown me.

Great waves would often flood me,
wash clean away my life.
Such peril in my journeys,
hardship, trouble, strife.

Adrift upon the oceans,
no anchor to a shore.
How long will I keep floating,
God calm my storms implore.

You may have stood and watched,
the roughness of my sea.
The storms were never ending,
kept trying to drown me.

Caught trapped in endless current,
no tiller for my steer.
Rudderless and oar-less,
just me alone with fear.

You stand upon your dry rock,
safe from the waves reach.
Certain in your knowledge,
sure I'll sink or beach.

You may have stood and watched,
the roughness of my sea.
The storms were never ending,
kept trying to drown me.

Onwards goes my journey,
struggle fight i keep to bail.
Refuse the lure of deepness,
continue i to sail.

Have you courage yet to join me,
join deck and help me sail.
Are you rudder lost returning,
success to stop my fail.

You may have stood and watched,
the roughness of my sea.
The storms were never ending,
kept trying to drown me.

Will you stand and always wonder,
blind to horizons glare.
Missed chance of great adventure,
because you wouldn't dare.

Your love could be the anchor,
safe harbour for my soul.
The rudder, sail and riggings,
to make my vessel whole.

You may have stood and watched,
the roughness of my sea.
The storms were never ending,
kept trying to drown me.

Come join me on the journey,
don't let the moment slip.
Turn flimsy single sailor,
make unsinkable my ship.

Don't stand on dock in yearning,
watch slow the fade from view.
Come leap and grasp what's passing,
it's all you have to do.

Together we'll calm waters,
and sail the seventh sea.
Those storms so never ending,
at last will set me free.

121. Captured dreams.

Did you catch me sneaking glances,
I didn't mean to stare.
Captured by a day dream,
running fingers through your hair.

I've never seen such beauty,
you melt me with your smile.
Your sweetness overwhelms me,
such elegance and style.

I really want to kiss you,
hold you close and tight.
See you in the moonbeams,
naked in the night.

Your smile it just melts me,
yet freezes still my heart.
I have so much I want to say,
just don't know how to start.

Did you catch me sneaking glances,
I didn't mean to stare.
Captured by a day dream,
running fingers through your hair.

Your perfume smells like Angels,
with fairy dust mixed in.
You smiled and said hello to me,
why won't my words begin.

I really want to kiss you,
hold you close and tight.
See you in the moonbeams,
naked in the night.

Such beauty leaves me dumb struck,
I'm lost so deep in awe.
Your eyes they hypnotise me,
and leave me wanting more.

Sweet lips do they invite me,
now hesitate the haste.
Saviour precious moments,
the longing me to taste.

So close I hear your breathing,
the thumping of your heart.
My hands caress your neckline,
at the first kiss that we start.

Did you catch me sneaking glances,
I didn't mean to stare.
Captured by a day dream,
running fingers through your hair.

So soft the tongue does flicker,
the gentle brush of lip.
My hand that traces lightly,
the curve and sway of hip.

I really want to kiss you,
hold you close and tight.
See you in the moonbeams,
naked in the night.

Intensify the passions,
how lust can quicken pace.
I close my eyes each night time,
just to see your face.

You fill my world with day dream,
my nights in fantasy.
Did you catch me sneaking glances,
why would you notice me.

Such lovely apparition,
a vision to behold.
The first time that I saw you,
the memory coated gold.

So sweet, so pure and perfect,
is the vision I see true.
Oh how I long for destiny,
to bring to me a you.

Did you catch me sneaking glances,
I didn't mean to stare.
Captured by a day dream,
running fingers through your hair.

We all of us see faces,
that take our breath away.
The souls of searched for lovers,
we look for every day.

I really want to kiss you,
hold you close and tight.
See you in the moonbeams,
naked in the night.

They stop our hearts with glances,
lift spirits with a smile.
Leave us lost in day dreams,
brief moments slowed a while.

How perfect are the moments,
each dream I take of you.
The shooting stars I wish upon,
to make the day dreams true.

Did you catch me sneaking glances,
I didn't mean to stare.
Captured by a day dream,
running fingers through your hair.

122. Is it me?

Is it me that's stirring passions,
when you lay in bed alone.
Your gentle touch of fingers,
exploring tender zone.

See how your legs do tremble,
lost all words to speak.
Intensify the moment,
my name in whispered speak.

How frantic does your pulse race,
what heaves your bosom high.
So hard the final climax,
how long your silent sigh.

Is it me that's stirring passions,
when you lay in bed alone.
Your gentle touch of fingers,
exploring tender zone.

Your body locked in spasms,
delectable delight.
Such intensity the moments,
the tender play this night.

Is it me that comes to haunt you,
every time you sleep and dream.
These new things that you're feeling,
Such lust that's never been.

Is it me that's stirring passions,
when you lay in bed alone.
Your gentle touch of fingers,
exploring tender zone.

Does a thought of me excite you,
send tingles to your toes.
Are the lost in day dream moments,
all taking off my clothes.

Are there moments in the shower,
The reasons you can't say.
When I drift into your fantasy,
and start your hands to play.

Is it me that's stirring passions,
when you lay in bed alone.
Your gentle touch of fingers,
exploring tender zone.

Do you think of me whilst touching,
your secret magic place.
Do you close your eyes in climax,
just to see my face.

How long the moment lingers,
passion spent and all subdued.
Do you think of me whilst touching,
why Madam, how rather rude.

123. Bitter rides resentment.

How bitter rides resentment,
when Devils drive the dream.
All moments lost forever,
the things that could have been.

Are we punished for a past life,
or doomed by future deed.
What purpose to existence,
does the world for me have need.

The loss of understanding,
all empathy is drained.
So close to acts of madness,
eternity be famed.

How bitter rides resentment,
when Devils drive the dream.
All moments lost forever,
the things that could have been.

I hear the little laughter's,
and daggers eyes i throw.
The simmer beneath the surface,
my volcanic tempt to blow.

I'll tear the world asunder,
smite out, destroy and burn.
The evils sweet persuasion,
his tempt a power yearn.

How bitter rides resentment,
when Devils drive the dream.
All moments lost forever,
the things that could have been.

Oh God above please save me,
spare redemptions soul.
Stop the stumble into darkness,
keep the spirit whole.

Please rid the fear and loathing,
wash clean a hearts contempt.
Lead to your salvation,
light up what darkness sent.

How bitter rides resentment,
when Devils drive the dream.
All moments lost forever,
the things that could have been.

124. Feel the sadness

Feel the sadness,
inside deep.
Dear old Grandpa,
now God's to keep.

The loss and pain,
our hearts must bare.
Empty slippers,
beneath the chair.

For all my life,
you shared your heart.
Right to the end,
from distant start.

Words of wisdom,
laughs and joke.
The world now robbed,
of one top bloke.

I remember when,
I was three.
I barely reached up,
to your knee.

You'd pick me up,
and lift me high.
I'd fly like Angels,
in the sky.

Feel the sadness,
inside deep.
Dear old Grandpa,
now God's to keep.

The loss and pain,
our hearts must bare.
Empty slippers,
beneath the chair.

Birthday moments,
of me aged six.
My broken bike,
that you did fix.

How I wish,
I could have again.
My Grandpa hugs,
when I was ten.

Christmas magic,
that you made last.
Even once,
I'd fourteen past.

Our fun and laughter,
each every day.
Such magic moments,
in memory stay.

Feel the sadness,
inside deep.
Dear old Grandpa,
now God's to keep.

The loss and pain,
our hearts must bare.
Empty slippers,
beneath the chair.

Words of wisdom,
knowledge shared.
We always knew,
you loved and cared.

Broken hearts,
that we endure.
Grandpa had,
the secret cure.

Stories told,
of things he'd done.
Hardships faced,
and battles won.

You made us smile,
filled eyes with laugh.
Kept all steady,
along life's path.

Feel the sadness,
inside deep.
Dear old Grandpa,
now God's to keep.

The loss and pain,
our hearts must bare.
Empty slippers,
beneath the chair.

For Grandpa now,
a top award.
His life of love,
has God's reward.

The Angels came,
gently took your hand.
Lead you above,
to the promised land.

You leave behind,
your love for all.
The trumpets sound,
throughout the hall.

Goodbye dear Grandpa,
farewell with love.
We know you watch us,
from clouds above.

Feel the sadness,
inside deep.
Dear old Grandpa,
now God's to keep.

The loss and pain,
our hearts must bare.
Empty slippers,
beneath the chair.

125. Memory clings to moments

My heart it hasn't realized,
your soul has left this world.
My memory clings to moments,
around me your arms curled.

The echoes of your laughter,
they sound from corners dark.
My spirits devastation,
such loss the lonely stark.

The tears they still surprise me,
slow fade from view your trace.
Daily comes reminders,
all shadows hide your face.

My mind it hasn't realized,
your soul has left this world.
My memory clings to moments,
around me your arms curled.

In moments lost in daydream,
I forget I'm left alone.
I find myself sat smiling,
texting you by phone.

The sadness then it hits me,
the pain and loss won't end.
No longer can you save me,
my shattered dreams to mend.

My spirit it hasn't realized,
your soul has left this world.
My memory clings to moments,
around me your arms curled.

126. My heart has cried

The pain it hurts,
so deep inside.
Between each beat,
my heart has cried.

Disbelief,
my distant stare,
snatched away,
my constant care.

Lost from me,
oh precious one.
What shall I do,
without you mum.

Throughout my life,
across the years.
You flooded love.
and dried my tears.

The pain it hurts,
so deep inside.
Between each beat,
my heart has cried.

I feel so lost,
my words can't say.
I thought forever,
that you would stay.

Sean Michael McCarthy

Remember when,
I was three,
You helped me climb,
that great big tree.

Great family days,
of Sunday dinner.
All races ran,
you made me winner.

The pain it hurts,
so deep inside.
Between each beat,
my heart has cried.

When I was 10,
you let me choose.
Those Doc Mart boots,
as my school shoes.

You sang me songs,
and lullaby.
Fails didn't matter,
so long the try.

My first broke heart,
at aged 14.
How sad my world,
did back then seem.

The pain it hurts,
so deep inside.
Between each beat,
my heart has cried.

Always there,
with welcome arms.
Protect from life,
with all its harms.

Goodbye to Mother,
farewell dear Mum.
Sleep in peace,
your job well done.

The pain it hurts,
so deep inside.
Between each beat,
my heart has cried.

I'll stare at stars,
the dark night sky.
Come cloud the moon,
don't see me cry.

I'll see the sun,
bright skies blue.
My silent moments,
now filled with you.

My ever rock,
where now you hide.
Submerged from view,
by passing tide.

The pain it hurts,
so deep inside.
Between each beat,
my heart has cried.

127. Legends our eyes see

We often fail to notice,
legends our eyes see.
Attentions get distracted,
by things we try to be.

The heroes of our childhood,
their rescue songs they sang.
Gone to quick the life they lived,
quick flash, then over, Bang!

Old words of inspiration,
in memory box long hid.
Quick wipe to blow the dust off,
the gentle lift of lid.

Beneath the fading photo's,
with yellow corners curled.
Old lyrics once with meaning,
to which we once hearts hurled.

We often fail to notice,
legends our eyes see.
Attentions get distracted,
by things we try to be.

The crackle pop of vinyl,
the smooth trace feels the scratch.
The frantic hunt of bed under,
and lift of attic hatch.

We find such precious memory,
those songs that saved our soul.
Was written words intention,
achieved did you the goal.

The ghosts we hid in corners.
your lyrics bound them tight.
You kept away all monsters,
that hunted us as night.

We often fail to notice,
legends our eyes see.
Attentions get distracted,
by things we try to be.

The words to us gave meaning,
smiles we count with tears.
How and why what reasons,
lay hid for all these years.

You hid in faded memory,
not seen but always there.
I'm sorry that I forgot you,
and how you use to care.

It's not 'til Angles claim you,
that we finally all awake.
And realise with hindsight,
the difference you did make.

We often fail to notice,
legends our eyes see.
Attentions get distracted,
by things we try to be.

Your music was hypnotic,
gave comfort cured all dread.
The burden was it heavy,
is it lifted now you're dead?

It's sad that you have left us,
this world now feels alone.
The years I failed to see you,
for that I will atone.

I'll listen to your music,
all the words that you us told.
And keep those faded memories,
dust free now coated gold.

We often fail to notice,
legends our eyes see.
Attentions get distracted,
by things we try to be.

Sean Michael McCarthy

128. Frantic grasps

Your eyes are pools of beauty,
so deep the drag me in.
I love the way a smile,
places dimple on your chin.

To hear your music laughter,
contention of your sighs.
So radiant the sparkle,
those rainbows in your eyes.

The warm glow from our love make,
the frantic grasp for air.
The plea for just one moment,
I brush from face your hair.

The heaving bosoms rhythm,
so quick begins to slow.
Amazing is the magic,
once out continue flow.

Can this really be the feeling,
of amazement never felt.
Eyes wide with wonder looking,
smile back from me is dealt.

You're holder of the magic,
it's inside you deep within.
Have you rested now my baby,
can I once again begin.

So slow trace I my kisses,
down neck, then shoulder, hip.
Each brush so light enticing,
tingles shock from brush of lip.

Fingers claw the linen duvet,
expectant arch of back.
Pulse is through the ceiling,
fingers nail and scratch my back.

Shudder shock explosions,
moist tongue in gentle swirl.
Like Queen of oceans oyster,
reveal to me your pearl.

Your panting breath so rapid,
my hair your grasp so tight.
Are you reaching super nova,
do you think explode you might.

The moment comes to catch you,
such timing un-aware.
The silence of not breathing,
oxygen is just not there.

The weep you give like crying,
but tears they glisten bliss.
See I told you there was magic,
inside of you my Miss.

Palms flatten rumpled cool sheets,
fingers spread in moment froze.
The magic's still escaping,
see it wiggle out your toes.

You tell me I'm amazing,
to you what do I do.
Why nothing my sweet baby,
the miracle's in you.

Inside you is the magic,
it simmer shines below.
Just need the right magician,
release that starburst flow.

Your eyes are pools of beauty,
so deep the drag me in.
I love the way a smile,
places dimple on your chin.

To hear your music laughter,
contention of your sighs.
So radiant the sparkle,
those rainbows in your eyes.

The warm glow from our love make,
the frantic grasp for air.
The plea for just one moment,
I brush from face your hair.

We lay in naked wonder,
bodies hot with warming glow.
Shall we once more take the journey,
this time fast not slow.

Your gasped amaze of startle,
what more, again, right now.
I smile my re-assurance,
gentle kiss upon your brow.

I'll show you how the magic,
continues with it's flow.
You'll reach the highest heavens,
places never did you go.

My kisses soft and tender,
they slowly close your eyes.
Only heavens Angels surely,
hear such happy sighs.

Fingers through your soft hair,
like velvet feels the trace.
Nuzzled flicks of tongues touch,
leaving kisses on your face.

Hands trace all your corners,
each soft smooth length of thigh.
Fingers releasing wetness,
Oh God your whispered cry.

The rhythmic thrust you quicken,
I want you pleads your cry.
Slow deep the penetration,
feel the soar as Angels fly.

Your eyes are full of rainbows,
your soul and spirit too.
Like precious sparkle moon dust,
God what magic resides in you.

Crescendo comes the climax,
together we are one.
The world stops froze by moment,
the magic again has come.

Intensity of moment,
the smiling catch of eye.
The laughter now in sharing,
pure happiness the cry.

Limbs in perfect tangle,
collapsed we are in heap.
Total understanding,
no words the need to speak.

Your eyes are pools of beauty,
so deep the drag me in.
I love the way a smile,
places dimple on your chin.

To hear your music laughter,
contention of your sighs.
So radiant the sparkle,
those rainbows in your eyes.

The warm glow from our love make,
the frantic grasp for air.
The plea for just one moment,
I brush from face your hair.

Sean Michael McCarthy

129. Life of 50 years

Today my heart hides sadness,
I'm crying silent tears.
It would have been your birthday,
a life of 50 years.

You failed to last the distance,
no chime from last lap bell.
That straight was too demanding,
lay down, gave up, fell.

Oh Wesley you old Bastard,
you comic, fool and friend.
I hope you lay in soft hands,
happy ever after with your end.

A year ago you partied,
birthday number 49.
We began to think you'd make it,
and hoped that all was fine.

You kept the suffer silent,
met each of us with cheer.
Don't worry I'll make 50,
it's just another year.

The race in you was fading,
Grim Reaper closing near.
Bollox, sod it, had enough,
reaching for a beer.

Sat in grassy sunshine,
with darkness closing in.
Planning tonight's party,
in Heaven with a grin.

What do they do on birthdays,
up high in heavens halls.
Are parties there permitted,
do they allow exposure balls.

Will you dance with David Bowie,
run naked through the grass.
With painted bolts of lightening,
across your face and on your ass.

Today my heart hides sadness,
I'm crying silent tears.
It would have been your birthday,
a life of 50 years.

130. Once shared.

We had some magic moments,
once shared the same nice dream.
Do you smile at reminders memory,
on those magic moments been.

Remember summers camping,
and swimming in the sea.
Hours that we spent playing,
together, just you and me.

Those waves that sent us crashing,
knocked us over to our knees.
That frantic moments panic,
the cough, the splutter sneeze.

How about Christmas morning,
when Santa left a bike.
I taught you how to ride it,
stood to watch just how you'd like.

We had some magic moments,
once shared the same nice dream.
Do you smile at reminders memory,
on those magic moments been.

The many weekday mornings,
driving you to school.
The pretend you didn't know me,
in case it ruined your cool.

You brought to me some laughter,
brightened up the home.
Refreshing was the change you gave,
from those that liked to moan.

Summer sun was seldom,
but when shone we had some fun.
The big pool in the garden,
where whirlpool games were done.

The ride out on our cycles,
a jolly to the park.
Past the old man in his garden,
with his big dog that would bark.

We had some magic moments,
once shared the same nice dream.
Do you smile at reminders memory,
on those magic moments been.

The holiday of sunshine,
swimming all day long.
Snorkel chasing fishes,
to Crete we all had gone.

The trip to that old island,
oh boy it was so hot.
A cooling dip in ocean,
I remember all, the lot.

I wonder if you miss me,
am I a forgotten dream.
Have I faded into shadows,
like I'd never been.

Do you thing of me when riding,
your cycle through the park.
Does memory jump to my laugh,
when that dog does bark.

We had some magic moments,
once shared the same nice dream.
Do you smile at reminders memory,
on those magic moments been.

Do you miss the mash potato,
with cheese in snowy ball.
Who now is father figure,
to catch your every fall.

I hope I gave you moments,
happy shadows in your head.
My words of goodnight Princess,
when up you went for bed.

I think of you quite often,
and yes it makes me sad.
For 14 months of sunshine,
I was your Foster Dad.

Thank you for the laughter,
the love and the delight.
I hope that life is good for you,
and everything is right.

We had some magic moments,
once shared the same nice dream.
Do you smile at reminders memory,
on those magic moments been.

131. Silhouettes.

Like silhouettes of sunshine,
you always brought good cheer.
See how the skies feel cloudy,
now you no longer here.

We find ourselves in moments,
lost deep reflective thought.
So vast the vacuum emptied,
stole of all you brought.

Too many are the memories,
when laughter split our side.
The darkness full of shadows,
lingers memory full of pride.

Madness under moonlight,
laughter in the sun.
Forever cherished moments,
all we shared and done.

Like silhouettes of sunshine,
you always brought good cheer.
See how the skies feel cloudy,
now you no longer here.

Farewell my friend so lovely,
the brightest spark of fire.
The love of life you showed us,
we forever, will all, admire.

We smile with your memory,
raise high the glass good cheer.
The empty space at table,
a you no longer here.

You're safe now up in heaven,
and shadows through the cloud.
Are cast by you and Angels,
when dancing is allowed.

Like silhouettes of sunshine,
you always brought good cheer.
See how the skies feel cloudy,
now you no longer here.

Sean Michael McCarthy

132. Little red hearts.

Little red hearts,
they fall to the floor.
As I open the card,
that came through the door.

Little red hearts,
they beat through the pain.
Bursting with hope,
to soon love again.

Little red hearts,
we all just have one.
Full of the memories,
of all we have done.

Little red hearts,
they slow nearly stop.
Where did you come from,
catch me I drop.

Little red hearts,
they fall to the floor.
As I open the card,
you sent through the door.

Little red hearts,
beats faded and weak.
The joy of true love,
abandoned the seek.

Little red hearts,
once full hear the sing.
How deep stabs the hurt,
the broke life can bring.

Little red hearts,
a flutter and skip.
The beat runs much faster,
from brush of your lip.

Little red hearts,
they fall to the floor.
As I open the card,
you sent through the door.

Little red hearts,
how quick they can mend.
When along comes a lover,
that special a friend.

Little red hearts,
lift spirits high.
New burst that now fills you,
soothing love sigh.

Little red hearts,
when full of love pure.
For all of life's worries,
so simple the cure.

As I open the card,
you sent through the door.
Little red hearts,
they fall to the floor.

Sean Michael McCarthy

133. Heard a whisper.

Today I heard a whisper,
someone called your name.
I looked in their direction,
but the face was not the same.

The call was for another,
a soul I did not know.
The memories again are stirring,
a tear breaks out to flow.

The moment freezes movements,
time is held glass still.
Fresh comes floods of sadness,
swallows bitter pill.

Empty stands the shadow,
once rich it coloured hearts.
How long can pain keep stabbing,
caught unaware when starts.

Today I heard a whisper,
someone called your name.
Reflex brings the wonder,
smile to counter pain.

Your soul that dwells in heaven,
closure reward to your plight.
Moments shared in history,
haunt my dreams at night.

Days they slip by silent,
time lost not realised.
Events and life still living,
keep feelings hid disguised.

But sometimes comes a moment,
stops still and froze mid stride.
A prompt to jog the memory,
release the things we hide.

The loss of things for sharing,
the air, the sun, the sky.
The questions thrown to Angels,
of why you had to die.

I heard a word called Wesley,
smiled right through the pain.
Today I heard a whisper,
someone called your name

134. Distant seems the memory.

How memories shorten miles

So distant seems the memory,
how fast now fades the dream.
Mind tricks has time elapsing,
all the places we have been.

Hear the echo of shared laughter,
the smiles that warm me still.
My heart so full to over burst,
yet thirst for more I will.

The burdens of a broken soul,
in endless struggle fight.
Lifted, swept away and gone,
you loved my heart alight.

A father without children,
is just another man.
Stripped bare of all adventure,
dreams robbed no longer can.

My focal point and centre,
the names throughout my rock.
I count the miles and minutes,
stare down, stop still the clock.

Scant pass goes time that tore us,
count tally hours since final part.
When I left you I stopped being,
and abandoned you my heart.

Your love tells me the fable,
of all I could have been.
So distant seems the memory,
how fast now fades the dream.

Ashlee Brooke you are my first born,
little Maddison our rose.
Ben was once the little man,
see now how fast he grows.

To count out days in tear drops,
how memories shorten miles.
This separation hardship,
this life with it's hard trials.

Sean Michael McCarthy

The magic moments captured,
forever saved to screen.
Those pictures showing places,
and all that we have been.

We walked around in sunshine,
see how happy shine our eyes.
When left alone at airports,
who hears a Daddies cries.

The miles I count ten thousand,
shared dream another world.
Such loss and lonely heartbreak,
pieces happy shattered hurled.

I'm lost without my children,
feel empty, cold inside.
Behind this brave face happy,
the hermit, recluse hide.

Each step I take a minute,
time closer and nearer you.
I know deep down inside me,
the things i have to do.

Climb mountains, chase down rainbows,
wade through the deepest sea.
Lay down the final jigsaw piece,
my children complete the me.

The path I now see clearly,
make so what should have been.
So distant seems the memory,
how fast now fades the dream.

135. That was our Nan.

That shooting star,
night sky span.
Heaven bound,
that was our Nan.

The Angels came,
they took your hand.
Lead you now,
sweet promised land.

You take our love,
small piece of heart.
The smile through tears,
from loves depart.

For all our lives,
always there.
Comfort words,
the time to care.

From scrape to knee,
love failed plan.
Smiles and hugs,
that was our Nan.

The silver moon,
so bright in sky.
Spotlights path,
the chose to die.

The Angels sing,
a glory song.
Such soft white wings,
to bare along.

Sean Michael McCarthy

You leave us here,
to smile through tears.
So many ghosts,
of memory years.

We'll search the sky,
each night we can.
That twinkle new,
that was our Nan.

You still shine down,
on all the world.
Around crying hearts,
you arms are curled.

The happy tears,
from loss of joy.
No time will fade,
or love destroy.

Your empty chair,
will fill the room.
Your soul now Gods,
the take too soon.

He is the master,
the grand his plan.
His newest Angel,
that was our Nan.

136. Away from harm.

Not forgotten,
never gone.
Around the corner,
away from harm.

Years may pass,
but remembered day.
You chose to leave,
and slipped away.

Left us all,
with questions why.
Hearts so heavy,
with questioned cry.

We lie to close,
shut tight our eyes.
Trick our hearts,
that no one dies.

Just left the room,
or exit stage.
It keeps suppressed,
our anguished rage.

The memory ghost,
who's shape is you.
Keeps fresh in mind,
all we did do.

The magic times,
all laughs we shared.
Your shake of hand,
that showed you cared.

We all pretend,
that you've not gone.
Just around the corner,
away from harm.

We've many friends,
and family too.
Who share that cloud,
sit next to you.

Mums and Dads,
Gramps and Nan.
Look after them,
do all you can.

Show them the way,
the secret trick.
Teach Angels ghost,
besides us stick.

Let them watch,
our strides through life.
Show them all joys,
protect from strife.

It's hard to know,
just how to say.
The loss feels fresh,
come this one day.

This day was once,
so full of mirth.
The celebrate,
your day of birth.

We raise our glass,
with cheers the charm.
Just around the corner,
away from harm.

Sean Michael McCarthy

137. Turned to Dust.

Will your lifetime even matter,
when your bones have turned to dust.
How fast the magic memories,
wither, fade and rust.

The echo's of lost laughter,
weakened fail to stay.
An image of your smiling face,
ghosting by away.

Will people even notice,
now sits the empty chair.
Conversations skirt the fact,
of you no longer there.

What difference does one light make,
once faded from the room.
See how they fail to notice,
hearts closed off so soon.

Insignificant the effort,
the time you took to give.
The many deeds Samaritan,
to help survive and live.

The shrug off of departed,
friend the same as foe.
Is bother too much hassle,
why does empathy not show.

Is a person judged by uses,
no matter once they've gone.
Turn you such the cold shoulder,
switch off that light that shone.

Such sorrow of reflection,
dismissed in blink of eye.
Does that lifetime now not matter,
now the gone to die.

The spirits swirl in anger,
dismay the dis-belief.
The hours they gave in counsel,
each turn of your new leaf.

You act as if no matter,
a tear refuse to part.
Not one deep sigh or shudder,
released from feel of heart.

Departs the souls of lost ones,
the gentle pull to sky.
The rain drops falling slowly,
each one a tear they cry.

The strings of love that held them,
stretch tight to final bust.
Will your lifetime even matter,
when your bones have turned to dust.

138. Reasons so uncertain.

The horrors that start swirling,
so deep within the mind.
With reasons so uncertain,
the cause we cannot find.

The strip away of normal,
attack of peace within.
Our world is turned upside down,
raped sanity begin.

The Devil comes a riding,
guns blazing into town.
Demonic scatter henchmen,
lasso and drag you down.

The shadow of the screaming soul,
fast shades a heart so black.
Shudder exhausts the final breathe,
within the drowning sack.

Slow motion drift to bottom,
such cold to suck the bone.
Spirit once so full of life,
now empty feels alone.

Colours pale the fade to dark,
sparkle lost to night.
Rainbows deep once full allure,
crumble black and white.

Beauty seen that filled the world,
now poisoned turned to rust.
Footsteps once in skip along,
trails all blown to dust.

Tunes to words in song to sing,
now bring a tear to eye.
How quick this wonder life can fail,
how fast can magic die.

Skies once blue and full of sun,
Quick gather stormy cloud.
Air once crisp and crystal clear,
smother mutes the Reapers shroud.

Comes pounce the doom in silent stealth,
the warning never heard.
How lonely feeds upon despair,
our frantic drowning stirred.

Why dark depress this turn of thought,
who's shadow fills my heart.
Words of anger shouted fear,
what makes this madness start.

The step to shadow hide away,
so frightened of the light.
The yearn for arms that wrap around,
and words that hug me right.

Sean Michael McCarthy

Happy days that filled a heart,
now overflow the dread.
Memories of all things gone wrong,
echo loud inside my head.

Take a chance in new belief,
will Karma pay all debt.
So many souls that slip beneath,
the tears the broke have wept.

Oh dark despair please walk on by,
just once me overlook.
Banish dreams the sharp knife cut,
the pills that many took.

The Devils dance across the heart,
jealous envy fills his soul.
Drag you down destroy what's good,
his purpose, mission, goal.

Keep tight my grip on final straw,
stay chase that rainbow end.
Lift gaze to stars that shine with love,
pray me an Angel send.

Guardian hand to steady hold,
lift keep me free of pit.
That dark abyss of strong drag down,
please see me free of it.

I yearn to stand out in the light,
warm sunshine on my face.
Life of laughter, joy and love,
God grant me please such grace.

The horrors that start swirling,
so deep within the mind.
With reasons so uncertain,
the cause we cannot find.

139. Precious memories.

When loved ones leave,
we can but strive.
Precious memories,
to keep alive.

Magic moments,
that fill our hearts.
Impulse a tear,
squeezed from our hearts.

Remember back,
to when I had.
Best friend buddy,
my dear old Dad.

Always there,
he stood with pride.
That run along,
first bike beside.

Taught me all,
that I now know.
Claimed by Angels,
his time to go.

Sometimes ponder,
trick of mind.
I wonder why,
my Dad can't find.

I look to heaven,
stars and moon.
Why did the Lord,
claim so soon.

The years drift by,
in endless haze.
Memory grasps,
past happy days.

Maybe gone,
no longer here.
Worry not,
when see the tear.

I am not sad,
But cry the joy.
Be proud of me,
your little boy.

I know through soul,
we'll never part.
The love you gave,
flows through my heart.

So here's to you,
upon this day.
Another year past,
since your slip away.

Precious memories,
to keep alive.
When loved ones leave,
we can but strive.

Sean Michael McCarthy

3. The clock screams - inspired by my personal battle with depression and beating it.

31. Cheek pressed into grass - inspiration arrived whilst watching the sad news on British soldiers killed in Afghan being returned and the funeral procession through the streets.

33. Rumbo - written for my cousin Robin who was so cruelly taken by a motorbike accident aged 38.

36. Winter fun - waking up to deep snow in Feb 2009 which was very rare for our seaside town.

43. Sitting on my bedroom floor - Me missing my children who had all moved to Australia.

49. Innocent play - memories of my children when they were little kept me going through the dark days of missing them so much.

51. Sparkle in my eye - was written for and read out at my wedding [hindsight now laughs at me for it].

55. Dear Daddy - an old school mate lost his Dad to cancer.

54. Inspiration flutters by - a young local girl known for her charity work passed away suddenly and unexpectedly and many young people in the town of Ilfracombe were affected.

58. Forgotten - my feelings of not being wanted or appreciated or loved.

64. There comes a time - written on the death of one of my oldest and best school mates Wesley who was taken too soon at the age of 49. I read this poem at his funeral service at the request of his family.

77. What words - A friend was struggling to know what to say to another friend who's partner was taken suddenly so I wrote this for her.

78. Grim reaper soul seeker - this arrived in the middle of a night shift when I saw a hedgehog with a death wish run into the jaws of a fox.

82. The world through rainbow tears - I wrote this whilst waiting in a Doctors surgery. A young mother was struggling to keep her autistic son quiet and other people showed no understanding or patience. I have an autistic son myself and wanted to express the pure innocence of how his mind might be working.

85. The pit - the daily battle many face to outrun and avoid or escape depression.

96. These thoughts, these thoughts - The turmoil inside my own head following the breakdown of my marriage.

99. Will Angels wings - one of 12 written in the week following my dear John letter announcing the end of my marriage, self therapy to stave off the slip into The Pit.

113. The biting words of winter - this arrived whilst out on patrol in the moonlight with the temperature at minus 3.

123. Bitter rides resentment - an attempt to explain the battle against demons one of my best friend fights every day, [he said that it was almost like I could read the pictures and pain inside his head].

127. Legends our eyes see - inspired by the very sad news of the passing of David Bowie, a musician I had grown up listening to and admiring.

132. Little red hearts - this arrived when I received and opened a Valentine card and loads of little glitter red hearts fell out of the envelope.

138. Reasons so uncertain - arrived after a night of turbulent dreams following the horror events in Belgium.

Printed in the United States
By Bookmasters

Printed in the United States
By Bookmasters